THE
OTHER
GOSPELS

THE OTHER GOSPELS

Non-Canonical Gospel Texts

Edited by
Ron Cameron

The Westminster Press
Philadelphia

Copyright © 1982 Ron Cameron

Book Design by Alice Derr

First edition

Published by The Westminster Press®
Philadelphia, Pennsylvania

PRINTED IN THE UNITED STATES OF AMERICA
9 8 7 6 5 4 3 2 1

Library of Congress Cataloging in Publication Data

Main entry under title:

The Other gospels.

  Bibliography: p.
  1. Apocryphal books (New Testament) I. Cameron, Ron.
II. Title.
BS2851.O83   1982   229'.8052   82-8662
ISBN 0-664-24428-9 (pbk.)   AACR2

For
Mark and Tim

Contents

Foreword

Since the end of the nineteenth century, numerous ancient Christian gospel writings have been discovered. A rich literature of this genre is thus known today. But for the student of the New Testament and the interested reading public, it has not always been easy to have access to these "other gospels"—and even much of New Testament scholarship is still carried on with little attention to this literature. Although these gospels were not accepted into the canon of the New Testament, they are, however, extremely important for the study of early Christianity, and they may yet substantially alter our concepts of ancient Christian history. Some would argue that these gospels add little to our picture of the historical Jesus. Our picture, however, is dependent upon our understanding of the transmission of traditions about and from Jesus and of the process of the formation of written gospel texts. The non-canonical gospels are important witnesses to these developments. In many instances, they are directly dependent upon the earliest stages of the collections of sayings of Jesus and stories about him; and they show little, if any, influence from the gospels of the New Testament. Students of early Christian literature will be greatly enriched if they utilize these materials as they learn to understand how the earliest oral traditions of Jesus were used and transformed in Christian communities: how they were collected, put into writing, edited, and repeatedly revised.

The non-canonical gospels demonstrate that this process by no means resulted exclusively in the composition of the four gospels of the New Testament. They establish further that this process did not come to an end with the New Testament. On the contrary, the four canonical gospels were still living documents, constantly used in the mission, instruction, and edification of Christian communities, and therefore, still subject to further development. As a result, more gospel writings continued to be produced, of which fragments still survive. While large parts of the early church finally limited the growth of this literature by canonizing the Gospels of Matthew, Mark, Luke, and John, other Christian groups continued to cultivate their own books— books which claim to contain both the genuine words of Jesus' revelation and their interpretations. Although some of these writings are known as "gnostic gospels," which sometimes place Jesus' words into a post-resurrection situation, they often preserve older traditions. Perhaps more important, these gospels reveal to us the way in which Christians in different situations renewed the living voice of Jesus on the basis of such older traditions.

Much can be learned here, since the basis for future scholarship on the oral and written transmission of the entire tradition about Jesus is much broader than was believed a few decades ago. The work has only begun and there are yet more questions than answers. The easier the access to these important texts, the greater is the hope that our insights will increase through the fruits of the labors of many—of scholars, students, and laypersons alike. This volume is a significant step toward providing precisely that access. Its introductions are substantive yet non-technical, and are based on the most up-to-date insights of critical scholarship. The "other gospels" are a valid and vital part of the life and faith of the early Christians. They deserve a fair and unbiased hearing.

HELMUT KOESTER

Acknowledgments

This book has grown out of my research on the origins and developments of gospel literature. It is, in part, the product of frustration experienced as a student in not having a convenient collection, in inexpensive format, of the non-canonical gospels.

Without the support of Helmut Koester, who introduced me to the riches of all gospel texts and helped me establish a set of methodological questions with which to explore their treasures, this volume would not have been possible. At his recommendation I was able to undertake this project. He read various drafts of this manuscript with critical insight and consummate skill; the final draft has benefited immeasurably from his comments.

George MacRae and Stephen Emmel read and reread my translation of the *Apocryphon of James*; their sensitivity to the nuances of the Coptic language have been invaluable in helping to clarify many difficult readings in the text. Gary Bisbee, Jeremy Cott, Phil Sellew, and John Strugnell offered excellent editorial suggestions. Working sessions with David Frankfurter and Arthur Just never failed to provide lively, challenging debates.

Other friends and colleagues graciously provided me with bibliographic references and pre-publication copies of their own manuscripts: Harry Attridge, Bruce Corley, Arthur Dewey, Frank Fallon, William R. Farmer, Bentley Layton, Dieter Lührmann, Pheme Perkins, and Frank Williams. To them I extend my thanks. I also wish to express my appreciation to the staff of the Andover-Harvard Theological Library for their cheerful and able assistance. Special gratitude is due to Holly Hendrix and Peggy Hutaff, who read this manuscript with great care and offered suggestions with the gentlest of counsel. Their seasoned eyes, unusual patience, gifted learning, and trenchant criticisms have purged the text of numerous offenses.

Fifteen of the sixteen translations printed here are reprinted by permission from previously published texts. These translations have been accepted with only slight alterations in spelling and punctuation and occasional modifications in wording. Any changes were made solely for the sake of consistency and clarity. All textual signs have been standardized in accordance with common papyrological practice. The texts are conventionally divided for handy reference into chapter and verse divisions, page and line references, or fragment numbers. The names of the persons responsible for each translation are given at the conclusion of the introductions to each text. The translation of the *Apocryphon of James* is my own, published here for the first time.

Grateful acknowledgment is made to the following publishing houses for permission to reprint previously published material:

Lutterworth Press and The Westminster Press: Excerpts from *New Testament Apocrypha*, Volume I: *Gospels and Related Writings*, edited by Wilhelm Schneemelcher and Edgar Hennecke. English translation edited by R. McL. Wilson. Published in the U.S.A. by The Westminster Press, 1963. Copyright © 1959 J. C. B. Mohr (Paul Siebeck), Tübingen. English translation © 1963 Lutterworth Press. Excerpts from *New Testament Apocrypha*, Volume II: *Writings Relating to the Apostles; Apocalypses and Related Subjects*, edited by Wilhelm Schneemelcher and Edgar Hennecke. English translation edited by R. McL. Wilson. Published in the U.S.A. by The Westminster Press, 1965. Copyright © 1964 J. C. B. Mohr (Paul Siebeck), Tübingen. English translation © 1965 Lutterworth Press. Reprinted by permission.

Harper & Row, Publishers, Inc.: Excerpts from *The Nag Hammadi Library*, edited by James M. Robinson. Copyright © 1977 by E. J. Brill, Leiden, The Netherlands. Reprinted by permission of E. J. Brill and Harper & Row, Publishers, Inc.

Harvard University Press: Excerpts from *Clement of Alexandria and a Secret Gospel of Mark*, by Morton Smith. © Copyright 1973 by the President and Fellows of Harvard College. Reprinted by permission of Harvard University Press.

Textual Signs

[ ]   Square brackets indicate a lacuna in the manuscript. When the text cannot be reconstructed, three dots are placed within the brackets, regardless of the length of the lacuna; a fourth dot, if appropriate, may function as a period. Letters, words, or phrases placed within the brackets indicate the suggested reconstructions of the editors of the text.

< >   Pointed brackets indicate a correction by the editors of a scribal omission or error.

{ }   Braces indicate words or phrases in the manuscript which the editors consider erroneous or superfluous.

. . .   Three dots placed at the beginning or end of translated sections indicate a lacuna which cannot be reconstructed, regardless of its length. In some instances, three dots are used without square brackets to indicate a series of letters within the text which do not constitute a translatable unit.

( )   Parentheses indicate material supplied by the translators. Words or phrases placed within the parentheses indicate translational clarifications of the ambiguities of the text. The abbreviations "sing.," "pl.," and "fem.," placed within parentheses, stand for "singular," "plural," and "feminine," respectively.

(?)   A question mark enclosed within parentheses indicates uncertainty in editing or translating the text. In some instances, the text is too fragmentary to be positively reconstructed or too ambiguous to be clearly translated; in others, the text appears to be corrupt, and emendation or translation cannot be made with complete confidence.

Introduction

THE OTHER GOSPELS is an anthology of gospel literature that is not part of the New Testament but is of extreme importance for the study of the origins of Christianity. This book is designed to make available in English a collection of relevant non-biblical writings of the earliest Christians that preserve sayings of Jesus and stories about him.

In early Christianity, the memory of Jesus was alive in the traditions of worshiping communities which produced and preserved sayings in Jesus' name and stories attributed to him. Initially these sayings and stories were transmitted in spoken form; eventually they came to be set down in written gospel texts. Gradually some of these writings came to be selected for the "canon," the list of books that were considered to have special status and authority and thus were accepted as part of the Christian Bible. Scholars past and present have relied almost exclusively on the canonical gospels of the New Testament as witnesses to the sayings and deeds of Jesus. Non-canonical texts have been routinely regarded as less important, assumed to be dependent on or influenced by the New Testament. However, recent discoveries have given us reason to call these assumptions into question. The rapidly expanding body of literary evidence—much of it available for the first time—is enabling us to retest the discoveries of the past and see old truths in a new light. New critical analysis is providing the opportunity to examine more fully the history of the literature in which Jesus traditions were transmitted, since substantial non-canonical texts can now be used as primary sources to clarify the developments of gospel traditions.

The sixteen texts that follow constitute what remains of the non-canonical gospels from the first and second centuries. Many are preserved only in fragmentary form; the ravages of time and of the censor's pen have resulted in the scantiness of the sources. Frequently these fragments are extant solely in quotations of early church writers. These writers repeatedly cited the texts incorrectly, attributing quotations to the wrong sources. They regularly suppressed evidence as well, and interpreted what they did record in a biased manner. Their mistakes have led to countless difficulties in our attempts to isolate and identify correctly the gospels in which these quotations belong. There are a few gospel fragments which are on papyrus so poorly preserved that they are not included in this volume. Free-floating sayings or stories, which are not part of a particular text, are also omitted here; they are the subject of a monograph, not an anthology. Other texts that are called gospels are not included because they either were composed too late or belong to a different category of literature.

Just what is a gospel? Strict usage of the term "gospel" to designate a genre of literature about Jesus is complex and problematic. The original use of this term in the Christian tradition was technical, describing both the activity of Christian missionaries and the content of their proclamation. Not until the middle of the second century, in the works of the early church writer Justin, do we find this term employed for the first time to denote written documents that present sayings of and stories about Jesus. Ever since the latter half of that century, a great variety of religious writings have come to be called gospels. But the use of this term to characterize a genre is misleading, since all gospels comprise various types of literature. They encompass not only collections of sayings, miracle stories, birth legends, infancy narratives, passion narratives, and resurrection stories, but also apocalypses, revelation discourses, exegetical interpretations of the Jewish scriptures, theological treatises, speculative dialogues, homiletic meditations, and pseudo biographies. The four gospels that came to be included in the New Testament share several of these formal features; these gospels are also composed of distinct literary traditions which are equally attested in a number of disparate sources.

Since the canonical gospels themselves are complex literary entities, exhibiting the same compositional features as many other gospels, the criterion for the identification and definition of gospel literature is not canonicity. In seeking to isolate the indicators of a text that distinguish this genre, one needs, rather, to discern the sources behind the texts. It is here, in the sources that have been embedded in the texts, that we find, for the first time, traditions about Jesus presented in written form. Written collections of sayings and stories thus gave gospel traditions their first literary repository. By isolating collections of sayings and stories intertwined into various legendary accounts of Jesus' life and teaching, one can identify the sources of the gospels and delineate the history of the transmission of their traditions. All texts and portions thereof that can be so isolated are to be brought into any discussion of the historical developments of gospel literature. This must be done without regard to external titles given to the texts or one's theological opinions about such texts.

The title of a work is not a reliable guide to its genre. Many documents entitled "gospels" do not, in fact, belong to the group of texts that present sayings of and stories about Jesus. The *Gospel of Truth*, for example, tells of the joyous proclamation of knowledge which Jesus has brought, and is to be compared with writings such as Paul's Epistle to the Romans, which describe the need, means, and effects of salvation. The recently discovered portions of the *Gospel of Mani*, on the other hand, do not present Jesus traditions at all, but describe Mani's alleged revelations and call to be a world missionary. Documents such as these represent an extended use of the term "gospel" to characterize a wide variety of writings which are so designated because they were considered to be authoritative by a particular community.

One of the most vexing problems in the study of gospel literature is determining with any sort of precision the date of composition of a particular document. This is no less a problem in seeking to date the gospels of the New Testament than it is in dating the non-canonical gospels. There are, however, techniques available that permit one to suggest, with a reasonable degree of confidence, a plausible date of composition:

1. Form criticism provides a means of ascertaining the relative dating of discrete pieces of the tradition. Texts whose literary forms are relatively spare can generally be dated to a period earlier than those which exhibit a more elaborate, developed stage of the tradition.

2. Compositional parallels in the gospel tradition furnish additional evidence. When the history of a saying or story in one text can be paralleled in another whose development can be determined and to which a date can be assigned, then a contemporaneous date of composition can generally be given to both texts.

3. The role given to persons of authority, whose position in a particular community serves to authenticate its transmission of the tradition, supplies further confirmation of a likely date of composition. At a certain point in the history of early Christianity, communities began to appeal to revered figures of the past in order to legitimate the

traditions of their own groups. The period in which the community that fostered the Gospel of John began to revere the memory of the Beloved Disciple and Peter by looking to them as the guarantors of its traditions, for example, was most likely contemporary with the time when the community of the *Gospel of Thomas* began to esteem Thomas and James by appealing to them as authorities in the transmission of its traditions.

4. Literary dependence of one document upon another, datable one establishes the earliest possible date at which the dependent document was composed. Thus, the date of the composition of the Gospel of Matthew and the Gospel of Luke is later than that of the Gospel of Mark, since Mark was used by Matthew and Luke as a source of their respective writings.

5. When a text refers to historical events, the text must have been composed sometime during or after those events took place. The Gospel of Mark's reference to the destruction of the Temple in Jerusalem in 70 C.E., for example, means that this document in its final form could not have been composed before that time.

6. The existence of external witnesses to a text gives fairly reliable confirmation of at least the latest possible date of composition of the text. Such external attestations consist of datable manuscripts and of quotations and references in early church writers. It is to be noted that, in these quotations and references, non-canonical gospels are cited as frequently as canonical gospels are. The attestations do not support any artificial distinction between canonical and non-canonical (or "apocryphal") writings. Church writers referred to documents of both categories with equal regularity, even when these same writers may have rejected one particular gospel or another.

It would be desirable and appropriate to include the four gospels of the New Testament in this volume as well, making it a complete collection of all gospel texts. The economy of space, however, has made this impossible. But it should be remembered that the four gospels that gained admission into the canon are primarily gospels about Jesus. In many instances, the history of the transmission of the traditions of Jesus' sayings and stories is reflected most directly in what are now non-canonical gospels. Clearly, when significant documents emerge from what is generally considered to be a group of texts of minor importance, we must reassess our scholarly judgments and return to the texts as inquiring students.

In each of the introductions to the gospel texts that follow, I have tried to discuss the critical issues concerning the nature and significance of the text. These issues include the following: the title of the document; its external attestations, literary forms, and sources; the original language of the text; the language(s) in which the extant text is preserved; the date and place of composition; the date and place of discovery, publication, and conservation of the extant edition(s) of the text; and the text's influence and relevance for the study of gospel literature. For all these gospels, select annotated bibliographies have also been appended, in which information is provided about the original editions of the texts, available facsimile editions, best critical editions, and a few important scholarly discussions. These will enable the reader to continue to use the texts judiciously. The "other gospels" are worthy of careful study. I hope this collection will help stimulate the enthusiastic discussion that all gospel traditions so richly deserve.

TRADITIONS
OF SAYINGS
OF JESUS

The Gospel of Thomas

The Gospel of Thomas (Gos. Thom.) *is a collection of traditional wisdom sayings, parables, prophecies, and proverbs attributed to Jesus. The Coptic text of the* Gospel of Thomas *is a translation of an original Greek text, of which fragments of three different manuscripts were found at the turn of this century at Oxyrhynchus, Egypt, and published shortly thereafter. The earliest of these Greek fragments dates from ca. 200* C.E. *The existence of three different copies of the Greek text gives evidence of rather frequent copying of this gospel in the third century. Moreover, the fact that the* Gospel of Thomas *was repeatedly referred to by name in church writings of the third and fourth centuries confirms that it was widely read in the early church. The Coptic translation is the only complete version of the* Gospel of Thomas *extant today. It survives as one of fifty-two tractates that make up the remains of thirteen codices of a library that was buried in the fourth century and discovered in 1945 at Nag Hammadi, Egypt. It is the second of seven tractates of Codex II of this library, commonly known today as the Coptic Gnostic Library. The Coptic text, which was first published in 1959, is conserved in the Coptic Museum of Old Cairo. The three Greek fragments are conserved in the Bodleian Library, Oxford University; the British Library, London; and the Houghton Library, Harvard University.*

The Gospel of Thomas *seems to be based on smaller collected sequences of sayings, both oral and written, arranged according to similarity in form and linked together into the current collection. Most of the sayings begin with the simple introductory formula: "Jesus said." Authorship is attributed to Didymos Judas Thomas, who was revered in the early Syriac church as an apostle and twin brother of Jesus. The name "Thomas" may be used to locate the authority and secure the identity of the tradition of those communities which appealed to Thomas as their founder.*

The designation of these sayings as "the secret sayings which the living Jesus spoke," whose interpretation will enable one to "not experience death," indicates that the discernment of the meaning of these sayings of Jesus was believed to bring secret wisdom. These sayings were understood as those of the voice of divine Wisdom revealing herself. Their interpretation is crucial; recognizing their meaning, a matter of life and death. Fundamentally, therefore, the Gospel of Thomas is an esoteric book which, according to the catechetical instruction imparted in Saying 50, reveals one's origin ("the light"), identity ("elect" "children"), and destiny ("repose").

Most of the sayings in the Gospel of Thomas have parallels in the "synoptic" gospels of Matthew, Mark, and Luke in the New Testament. Analysis of each of these sayings reveals that the sayings in the Gospel of Thomas are either preserved in forms more primitive than those in the parallel sayings in the New Testament or are developments of more primitive forms of such sayings. The particular editorial changes which the synoptic gospels make, including the addition of a narrative structure and the inclusion of traditional sayings and stories within a biographical framework, are totally absent from the Gospel of Thomas. All of this suggests that the Gospel of Thomas is based on a tradition of sayings which is closely related to that of the canonical gospels but which has experienced a separate process of transmission. The composition of the Gospel of Thomas, therefore, is parallel to that of the canonical gospels. Its sources are collections of sayings and parables contemporary with the sources of the canonical gospels. In this respect, the Gospel of Thomas can be profitably compared with the Synoptic Sayings Source, common to Matthew and Luke, generally referred to as Q (from the first letter of the German word Quelle, meaning "source").

It is probable that many of the sayings in the Gospel of Thomas which are not preserved elsewhere also derive from early traditions of sayings of Jesus. This document is, therefore, an important source of as well as witness to Jesus' sayings. Since the Gospel of Thomas is independent of the writings of the New Testament, its date of composition is not contingent upon these or any other written documents we now possess. Its earliest possible date of composition would be in the middle of the first century, when other sayings collections first began to be compiled. The latest possible date would be at the end of the second century, shortly before the copies found at Oxyrhynchus were made and the first reference to the Gospel of Thomas was recorded by

Hippolytus (a church writer who lived at the beginning of the third century). Since the composition of the Gospel of Thomas parallels that of the gospels of the New Testament, the most likely date of its composition would be in the second half of the first century, almost certainly in Syria.

The text is divided according to the page and line numbers (32.10–51.28) of the Coptic manuscript. The numbering of these one hundred fourteen sayings is not given in any of the manuscripts, but is in accordance with scholarly practice. The translation was made by Thomas O. Lambdin (The Nag Hammadi Library).

The Gospel of Thomas

These are the secret sayings which the living Jesus spoke and which Didymos Judas Thomas wrote down.

(1) And he said, "Whoever finds the interpretation of these sayings will not experience death."

(2) Jesus said, [15] "Let him who seeks continue seeking until he finds. When he finds, he will become troubled. When he becomes troubled, he will be astonished, and he will rule over the All."

(3) Jesus said, "If [20] those who lead you say to you, 'See, the Kingdom is in the sky,' then the birds of the sky will precede you. If they say to you, 'It is in the sea,' then the fish will precede you. [25] Rather, the Kingdom is inside of you, and it is outside of you. When you come to know yourselves, then you will become known, [33] and you will realize that it is you who are the sons of the living Father. But if you will not know yourselves, you dwell in poverty and it is you [5] who are that poverty."

(4) Jesus said, "The man old in days will not hesitate to ask a small child seven days old about the place of life, and he will live. For many who are first will become last, [10] and they will become one and the same."

(5) Jesus said, "Recognize what is in your sight, and that which is hidden from you will become plain to you. For there is nothing hidden which will not become manifest."

(6) His disciples questioned Him [15] and said to Him, "Do You want

us to fast? How shall we pray? Shall we give alms? What diet shall we observe?"

Jesus said, "Do not tell lies, and do not do what you hate, for [20] all things are plain in the sight of Heaven. For nothing hidden will not become manifest, and nothing covered will remain without being uncovered."

(7) Jesus said, "Blessed is the lion which [25] becomes man when consumed by man; and cursed is the man whom the lion consumes, and the lion becomes man."

(8) And He said, "The man is like a wise fisherman [30] who cast his net into the sea and drew it up from the sea full of small fish. Among them the wise fisherman found a fine large fish. He threw [35] all the small fish **34** back into the sea and chose the large fish without difficulty. Whoever has ears to hear, let him hear."

(9) Jesus said, "Now the sower went out, took a handful (of seeds), [5] and scattered them. Some fell on the road; the birds came and gathered them up. Others fell on rock, did not take root in the soil, and did not produce ears. And others fell on thorns; [10] they choked the seed(s) and worms ate them. And others fell on the good soil and produced good fruit: it bore sixty per measure and a hundred and twenty per measure."

(10) Jesus said, "I have cast fire upon [15] the world, and see, I am guarding it until it blazes."

(11) Jesus said, "This heaven will pass away, and the one above it will pass away. The dead are not alive, and the living will not die. In the days when you consumed [20] what is dead, you made it what is alive. When you come to dwell in the light, what will you do? On the day when you were one you became two. But when you become two, what [25] will you do?"

(12) The disciples said to Jesus, "We know that You will depart from us. Who is to be our leader?"

Jesus said to them, "Wherever you are, you are to go to James the righteous, [30] for whose sake heaven and earth came into being."

(13) Jesus said to His disciples, "Compare me to someone and tell Me whom I am like."

Simon Peter said to Him, "You are like a righteous angel."

Matthew said to Him, **35** "You are like a wise philosopher."

Thomas said to Him, "Master, my mouth is wholly incapable of saying whom You are like."

Jesus said, [5] "I am not your master. Because you have drunk, you have become intoxicated from the bubbling spring which I have measured out."

And He took him and withdrew and told him three things. When Thomas returned to his companions, they asked him, [10] "What did Jesus say to you?"

Thomas said to them, "If I tell you one of the things which he told me, you will pick up stones and throw them at me; a fire will come out of the stones and burn you up." [15]

(14) Jesus said to them, "If you fast, you will give rise to sin for yourselves; and if you pray, you will be condemned; and if you give alms, you will do harm to your spirits. When you [20] go into any land and walk about in the districts, if they receive you, eat what they will set before you, and heal the sick among them. For what goes into your mouth [25] will not defile you, but that which issues from your mouth—it is that which will defile you."

(15) Jesus said, "When you see one who was not born of woman, prostrate yourselves on [30] your faces and worship him. That one is your Father."

(16) Jesus said, "Men think, perhaps, that it is peace which I have come to cast upon the world. They do not know that it is dissension which I have come to cast [35] upon the earth: fire, sword, and war. For there will be five 36 in a house: three will be against two, and two against three, the father against the son, and the son against the father. And they will stand solitary." [5]

(17) Jesus said, "I shall give you what no eye has seen and what no ear has heard and what no hand has touched and what has never occurred to the human mind."

(18) The disciples said to Jesus, "Tell [10] us how our end will be."

Jesus said, "Have you discovered, then, the beginning, that you look for the end? For where the beginning is, there will the end be. Blessed is [15] he who will take his place in the beginning; he will know the end and will not experience death."

(19) Jesus said, "Blessed is he who came into being before he came into being. If you become My disciples [20] and listen to My words, these stones will minister to you. For there are five trees for you in Paradise which remain undisturbed summer and winter and whose leaves do not fall. [25] Whoever becomes acquainted with them will not experience death."

(20) The disciples said to Jesus, "Tell us what the Kingdom of Heaven is like."

He said to them, "It is like a mustard seed, the smallest of [30] all seeds. But when it falls on tilled soil, it produces a great plant and becomes a shelter for birds of the sky."

(21) Mary said to Jesus, "Whom are Your disciples [35] like?"

He said, "They are like [37] children who have settled in a field which is not theirs. When the owners of the field come, they will say, 'Let us have back our field.' They (will) undress in their presence [5] in order to let them have back their field and to give it back to them. Therefore I say to you, if the owner of a house knows that the thief is coming, he will begin his vigil before he comes and will not let him dig through into his house of his [10] domain to carry away his goods. You, then, be on your guard against the world. Arm yourselves with great strength lest the robbers find a way to come to you, for the difficulty which you expect [15] will (surely) materialize. Let there be among you a man of understanding. When the grain ripened, he came quickly with his sickle in his hand and reaped it. Whoever has ears to hear, let him hear." [20]

(22) Jesus saw infants being suckled. He said to His disciples, "These infants being suckled are like those who enter the Kingdom."

They said to Him, "Shall we then, as children, enter the Kingdom?"

Jesus said to them, [25] "When you make the two one, and when you make the inside like the outside and the outside like the inside, and the above like the below, and when you make the male and the female one and the same, [30] so that the male not be male nor the female female; and when you fashion eyes in place of an eye, and a hand in place of a hand, and a foot in place of a foot, and a likeness in place of a likeness; [35] then will you enter [the Kingdom]." [38]

(23) Jesus said, "I shall choose you, one out of a thousand, and two out of ten thousand, and they shall stand as a single one."

(24) His disciples said to Him, "Show us the place [5] where You are, since it is necessary for us to seek it."

He said to them, "Whoever has ears, let him hear. There is light within a man of light, and he (or: it) lights up the whole world. If he (or: it) [10] does not shine, he (or: it) is darkness."

(25) Jesus said, "Love your brother like your soul, guard him like the pupil of your eye."

(26) Jesus said, "You see the mote in your brother's eye, but you do not see the beam in your own eye. When [15] you cast the beam out of your own eye, then you will see clearly to cast the mote from your brother's eye."

(27) ⟨Jesus said,⟩ "If you do not fast as regards the world, you will not find the Kingdom. If you do not observe the Sabbath as a Sabbath, [20] you will not see the Father."

(28) Jesus said, "I took My place in the midst of the world, and I appeared to them in flesh. I found all of them intoxicated; I found none of them thirsty. And My soul became afflicted [25] for the sons of men, because they are blind in their hearts and do not have sight; for empty they came into the world, and empty too they seek to leave the world. But for the moment they are intoxicated. [30] When they shake off their wine, then they will repent."

(29) Jesus said, "If the flesh came into being because of spirit, it is a wonder. But if spirit came into being because of the body, it is a wonder of wonders. Indeed, I am amazed [39] at how this great wealth has made its home in this poverty."

(30) Jesus said, "Where there are three gods, they are gods. Where there are two or one, I [5] am with him."

(31) Jesus said, "No prophet is accepted in his own village; no physician heals those who know him."

(32) Jesus said, "A city being built on a high mountain and fortified cannot fall, [10] nor can it be hidden."

(33) Jesus said, "Preach from your housetops that which you will hear in your ear {(and) in the other ear}. For no one lights a lamp and puts it under a bushel, nor does he put it in a [15] hidden place, but rather he sets it on a lampstand so that everyone who enters and leaves will see its light."

(34) Jesus said, "If a blind man leads a blind man, they will both fall [20] into a pit."

(35) Jesus said, "It is not possible for anyone to enter the house of a strong man and take it by force unless he binds his hands; then he will (be able to) ransack his house."

(36) Jesus said, "Do not be concerned from [25] morning until evening and from evening until morning about what you will wear."

(37) His disciples said, "When will You become revealed to us and when shall we see You?"

Jesus said, "When [30] you disrobe without being ashamed and take up your garments and place them under your feet like little children and tread on them, then [will you see] [40] the Son of the Living One, and you will not be afraid."

(38) Jesus said, "Many times have you desired to hear these words which I am saying to you, and you have [5] no one else to hear them

from. There will be days when you will look for Me and will not find Me."

(39) Jesus said, "The Pharisees and the scribes have taken the keys of Knowledge and hidden them. They themselves have not entered, [10] nor have they allowed to enter those who wish to. You, however, be as wise as serpents and as innocent as doves."

(40) Jesus said, "A grapevine has been planted outside of the Father, but being [15] unsound, it will be pulled up by its roots and destroyed."

(41) Jesus said, "Whoever has something in his hand will receive more, and whoever has nothing will be deprived of even the little he has."

(42) Jesus said, "Become passers-by." [20]

(43) His disciples said to him, "Who are You, that You should say these things to us?"

⟨Jesus said to them,⟩ "You do not realize who I am from what I say to you, but you have become like the Jews, for they (either) love the tree and hate [25] its fruit (or) love the fruit and hate the tree."

(44) Jesus said, "Whoever blasphemes against the Father will be forgiven, and whoever blasphemes against the Son will be forgiven, but whoever blasphemes against the Holy Spirit [30] will not be forgiven either on earth or in heaven."

(45) Jesus said, "Grapes are not harvested from thorns, nor are figs gathered from thistles, for they do not produce fruit. A good man brings forth 41 good from his storehouse; an evil man brings forth evil things from his evil storehouse, which is in his heart, and says evil things. For out of [5] the abundance of the heart he brings forth evil things."

(46) Jesus said, "Among those born of women, from Adam until John the Baptist, there is no one so superior to John the Baptist that his eyes should not be lowered (before him). [10] Yet I have said, whichever one of you comes to be a child will be acquainted with the Kingdom and will become superior to John."

(47) Jesus said, "It is impossible for a man to mount two horses or to stretch two bows. And it is impossible [15] for a servant to serve two masters; otherwise, he will honor the one and treat the other contemptuously. No man drinks old wine and immediately desires to drink new wine. And new wine is not put into old wineskins, [20] lest they burst; nor is old wine put into a new wineskin, lest it spoil it. An old patch is not sewn onto a new garment, because a tear would result."

(48) Jesus said, "If two make peace with [25] each other in this one house, they will say to the mountain, 'Move away,' and it will move away."

(49) Jesus said, "Blessed are the solitary and elect, for you will find the Kingdom. For you are from it, [30] and to it you will return."

(50) Jesus said, "If they say to you, 'Where did you come from?', say to them, 'We came from the light, the place where the light came into being on [35] its own accord and established [itself] **42** and became manifest through their image.' If they say to you, 'Is it you?', say, 'We are its children, and we are the elect of the Living Father.' If they ask you, [5] 'What is the sign of your Father in you?', say to them, 'It is movement and repose.' "

(51) His disciples said to Him, "When will the repose of the dead come about, and when [10] will the new world come?"

He said to them, "What you look forward to has already come, but you do not recognize it."

(52) His disciples said to Him, "Twenty-four prophets spoke in Israel, [15] and all of them spoke in You."

He said to them, "You have omitted the one living in your presence and have spoken (only) of the dead."

(53) His disciples said to Him, "Is circumcision beneficial or not?"

He said [20] to them, "If it were beneficial, their father would beget them already circumcised from their mother. Rather, the true circumcision in spirit has become completely profitable."

(54) Jesus said, "Blessed are the poor, for yours is the Kingdom of Heaven." [25]

(55) Jesus said, "Whoever does not hate his father and his mother cannot become a disciple to Me. And whoever does not hate his brothers and sisters and take up his cross in My way will not be worthy of Me." [30]

(56) Jesus said, "Whoever has come to understand the world has found (only) a corpse, and whoever has found a corpse is superior to the world."

(57) Jesus said, "The Kingdom of the Father is like a man who had [good] seed. [35] His enemy came by night **43** and sowed weeds among the good seed. The man did not allow them to pull up the weeds; he said to them, 'I am afraid that you will go intending to pull up the weeds [5] and pull up the wheat along with them.' For on the day of the harvest the weeds will be plainly visible, and they will be pulled up and burned."

(58) Jesus said, "Blessed is the man who has suffered and found life."

(59) Jesus said, "Take heed of the [10] Living One while you are alive, lest you die and seek to see Him and be unable to do so."

(60) ⟨They saw⟩ a Samaritan carrying a lamb on his way to Judea. He said to his disciples, "(Why does) that man (carry) the [15] lamb around?"

They said to Him, "So that he may kill it and eat it."

He said to them, "While it is alive, he will not eat it, but only when he has killed it and it has become a corpse."

They said to Him, "He cannot do so otherwise."

He said to them, [20] "You too, look for a place for yourselves within Repose, lest you become a corpse and be eaten."

(61) Jesus said, "Two will rest on a bed: the one will die, the other [25] will live."

Salome said, "Who are You, man, that You, as though from the One, (or: as ⟨whose son⟩, that You) have come up on my couch and eaten from my table?"

Jesus said to her, "I am He who exists from the Undivided. [30] I was given some of the things of My father."

⟨Salome said,⟩ "I am Your disciple."

⟨Jesus said to her,⟩ "Therefore I say, if he is ⟨undivided⟩, he will be filled with light, but if he is divided, he will be filled with darkness."

(62) Jesus said, "It [35] is to those [who are worthy of [44] My] mysteries that I tell My mysteries. Do not let your left hand know what your right hand is doing."

(63) Jesus said, "There was a rich man who had much money. He said, 'I shall put [5] my money to use so that I may sow, reap, plant, and fill my storehouse with produce, with the result that I shall lack nothing.' Such were his intentions, but that same night he died. Let him who has ears [10] hear."

(64) Jesus said, "A man had received visitors. And when he had prepared the dinner, he sent his servant to invite the guests. He went to the first one and said to him, 'My master invites [15] you.' He said, 'I have claims against some merchants. They are coming to me this evening. I must go and give them my orders. I ask to be excused from the dinner.' He went to another and said to him, 'My master has invited you.' [20] He said to him, 'I have just bought a house and am required for the day. I shall not have any spare time.' He went to another and said to him, 'My master invites you.' He said to him, 'My friend is going to get married, and I am to prepare the banquet. [25] I

shall not be able to come. I ask to be excused from the dinner.' He went to another and said to him, 'My master invites you.' He said to him, 'I have just bought a farm, and I am on my way to collect the rent. I shall not be able to come. I ask to be excused.' The servant returned and said [30] to his master, 'Those whom you invited to the dinner have asked to be excused.' The master said to his servant, 'Go outside to the streets and bring back those whom you happen to meet, so that they may dine.' Businessmen and merchants [35] will not enter the Places of My Father." 45   *whoa.*

(65) He said, "There was a good man who owned a vineyard. He leased it to tenant farmers so that they might work it and he might collect the produce from them. He sent his servant so that [5] the tenants might give him the produce of the vineyard. They seized his servant and beat him, all but killing him. The servant went back and told his master. The master said, 'Perhaps ⟨they⟩ did not recognize ⟨him⟩.' [10] He sent another servant. The tenants beat this one as well. Then the owner sent his son and said, 'Perhaps they will show respect to my son.' Because the tenants knew that it was he who was the heir [15] to the vineyard, they seized him and killed him. Let him who has ears hear."

(66) Jesus said, "Show me the stone which the builders have rejected. That one is the cornerstone."

(67) Jesus said, "Whoever believes that the All [20] itself is deficient is (himself) completely deficient."

(68) Jesus said, "Blessed are you when you are hated and persecuted. Wherever you have been persecuted they will find no Place." [25]

(69) Jesus said, "Blessed are they who have been persecuted within themselves. It is they who have truly come to know the Father. Blessed are the hungry, for the belly of him who desires will be filled."

(70) Jesus said, [30] "That which you have will save you if you bring it forth from yourselves. That which you do not have within you will kill you if you do not have it within you."

(71) Jesus said, "I shall destroy [this] house, [35] and no one will be able to rebuild it." 46

(72) [A man said] to Him, "Tell my brothers to divide my father's possessions with me."

He said to him, "O man, who has made Me a divider?"

He turned to [5] His disciples and said to them, "I am not a divider, am I?"

(73) Jesus said, "The harvest is great but the laborers are few. Beseech the Lord, therefore, to send out laborers to the harvest."

(74) He said, "O Lord, there are [10] many around the drinking trough, but there is nothing in the cistern."

(75) Jesus said, "Many are standing at the door, but it is the solitary who will enter the bridal chamber."

(76) Jesus said, "The Kingdom of the Father is like a [15] merchant who had a consignment of merchandise and who discovered a pearl. That merchant was shrewd. He sold the merchandise and bought the pearl alone for himself. You too, seek [20] his unfailing and enduring treasure where no moth comes near to devour and no worm destroys."

(77) Jesus said, "It is I who am the light which is above them all. It is I who am the All. [25] From Me did the All come forth, and unto Me did the All extend. Split a piece of wood, and I am there. Lift up the stone, and you will find Me there."

(78) Jesus said, "Why have you come out into the desert? To see a reed [30] shaken by the wind? And to see a man clothed in fine garments like your kings and your great [47] men? Upon them are the fine [garments], and they are unable to discern the truth."

(79) A woman from the crowd said to Him, "Blessed are the womb which [5] bore You and the breasts which nourished You."

He said to her, "Blessed are those who have heard the word of the Father and have truly kept it. For there will be days [10] when you will say, 'Blessed are the womb which has not conceived and the breasts which have not given milk.' "

(80) Jesus said, "He who has recognized the world has found the body, but he who has found the body is superior to the world." [15]

(81) Jesus said, "Let him who has grown rich be king, and let him who possesses power renounce it."

(82) Jesus said, "He who is near Me is near the fire, and he who is far from Me is far from the Kingdom."

(83) Jesus said, [20] "The images are manifest to man, but the light in them remains concealed in the image of the light of the Father. He will become manifest, but his image will remain concealed by his light."

(84) Jesus said, [25] "When you see your likeness, you rejoice. But when you see your images which came into being before you, and which neither die nor become manifest, how much you will have to bear!"

(85) Jesus said, [30] "Adam came into being from a great power and a great wealth, but he did not become worthy of you. For had he been worthy, [he would] not [have experienced] death."

(86) Jesus said, "[The foxes 48 have their holes] and the birds have [their] nests, but the Son of Man has no place to lay his head and rest."

(87) Jesus said, "Wretched 5 is the body that is dependent upon a body, and wretched is the soul that is dependent on these two."

(88) Jesus said, "The angels and the prophets will come to you and give to you those things you (already) have. And 10 you too, give them those things which you have, and say to yourselves, 'When will they come and take what is theirs?' "

(89) Jesus said, "Why do you wash the outside of the cup? Do you not realize that 15 he who made the inside is the same one who made the outside?"

(90) Jesus said, "Come unto Me, for My yoke is easy and My lordship is mild, and you will find repose for 20 yourselves."

(91) They said to Him, "Tell us who You are so that we may believe in You."

He said to them, "You read the face of the sky and of the earth, but you have not recognized the one who (or: that which) is before you, and 25 you do not know how to read this moment."

(92) Jesus said, "Seek and you will find. Yet, what you asked Me about in former times and which I did not tell you then, now I do desire to tell, but you do not inquire after 30 it."

(93) ⟨Jesus said,⟩ "Do not give what is holy to dogs, lest they throw them on the dung-heap. Do not throw the pearls to swine, lest they grind it [to bits]."

(94) Jesus [said], "He who seeks will find, and [he who knocks] will be let in." 35

(95) [Jesus said], "If you have money, 49 do not lend it at interest, but give [it] to one from whom you will not get it back."

(96) Jesus [said], "The Kingdom of the Father is like a certain woman. She took a little leaven, [concealed] it in 5 some dough, and made it into large loaves. Let him who has ears hear."

(97) Jesus said, "The Kingdom of the [Father] is like a certain woman who was carrying a jar full of meal. While she was walking [on] a road, 10 still some distance from home, the handle of the jar broke and the meal emptied out behind her on the road. She did not realize it; she had noticed no accident. When she reached her house, she set the jar down and found it 15 empty."

(98) Jesus said, "The Kingdom of the Father is like a certain man who wanted to kill a powerful man. In his own house he drew his sword and stuck it into the wall in order to find out whether his hand could carry through. 20 Then he slew the powerful man."

(99) The disciples said to Him, "Your brothers and Your mother are standing outside."

He said to them, "Those here who do the will of My Father are [25] My brothers and My mother. It is they who will enter the Kingdom of My Father."

(100) They showed Jesus a gold coin and said to Him, "Caesar's men demand taxes from us."

He said to them, "Give Caesar what belongs [30] to Caesar, give God what belongs to God, and give Me what is Mine."

(101) ⟨Jesus said,⟩ "Whoever does not hate his father and his mother as I do cannot become a disciple to Me. And whoever does [not] love his father and his [35] mother as I do cannot become a [disciple] to Me. For My mother [gave me falsehood], [50] but [My] true [Mother] gave me life."

⟶

(102) Jesus said, "Woe to the Pharisees, for they are like a dog sleeping in the manger of oxen, for neither does he eat [5] nor does he let the oxen eat."

(103) Jesus said, "Fortunate is the man who knows where the brigands will enter, so that he may get up, muster his domain, and arm himself [10] before they invade."

(104) They said [to Jesus], "Come, let us pray today and let us fast."

Jesus said, "What is the sin that I have committed, or wherein have I been defeated? But when the bridegroom leaves [15] the bridal chamber, then let them fast and pray."

(105) Jesus said, "He who knows the father and the mother will be called the son of a harlot."

(106) Jesus said, "When you make the two one, you will become [20] the sons of man, and when you say, 'Mountain, move away,' it will move away."

(107) Jesus said, "The Kingdom is like a shepherd who had a hundred sheep. One of them, the largest, went astray. [25] He left the ninety-nine and looked for that one until he found it. When he had gone to such trouble, he said to the sheep, 'I care for you more than the ninety-nine.' "

(108) Jesus said, "He who will drink from My mouth will become like Me. I myself shall become [30] he, and the things that are hidden will be revealed to him."

(109) Jesus said, "The Kingdom is like a man who had a [hidden] treasure in his field without knowing it. And [after] he died, he left it to his [35] son. The son did not know (about the treasure). He inherited [51] the field and sold [it]. And the one who bought it went plowing and

found the treasure. He began to lend money at interest to whomever he wished."

(110) Jesus said, "Whoever finds the world [5] and becomes rich, let him renounce the world."

(111) Jesus said, "The heavens and the earth will be rolled up in your presence. And the one who lives from the Living One will not see death." Does not Jesus say, "Whoever finds himself [10] is superior to the world"?

(112) Jesus said, "Woe to the flesh that depends on the soul; woe to the soul that depends on the flesh."

two become one ?

(113) His disciples said to Him, "When will the Kingdom come?" ⟨Jesus said,⟩ "It will not come by [15] waiting for it. It will not be a matter of saying 'Here it is' or 'There it is.' Rather, the Kingdom of the Father is spread out upon the earth, and men do not see it."

(114) Simon Peter said to them, "Let Mary leave us, [20] for women are not worthy of Life."

Jesus said, "I myself shall lead her in order to make her male, so that she too may become a living spirit resembling you males. For every woman who will make herself [25] male will enter the Kingdom of Heaven."

oh man

The Gospel
According to Thomas

The Dialogue of the Savior

The Dialogue of the Savior (Dial. Sav.) *is a complex and rather fragmentary document that preserves traditions of the sayings of Jesus in the form of a dialogue between Jesus and three of his disciples, Judas, Matthew, and Mariam. Originally written in Greek, the text is extant only in a Coptic translation. It is the last of five tractates that make up* Codex III *of the Coptic Gnostic Library from Nag Hammadi. Discovered in 1945, and first published in 1976, the document is conserved in the Coptic Museum of Old Cairo.*

The main source of the Dialogue of the Savior *is a dialogue based on a traditional collection of sayings. This dialogue is, in fact, simply an expanded sayings collection: individual sayings are cited as questions of the disciples, then expanded and interpreted through Jesus' replies. Many of the sayings underlying this source have parallels in Matthew, Luke, John, and, most of all, the* Gospel of Thomas. *The use of a sayings tradition comparable to these suggests that this dialogue source may have been composed in the second half of the first century* C.E.; *the close relationship among the* Dialogue of the Savior, *the* Gospel of Thomas, *and the* Gospel of John *makes it likely that this dialogue source also came from Syria. Moreover, the extraordinary number of parallels with the* Gospel of Thomas *permits the thesis that the* Dialogue of the Savior *directly continues the tradition of sayings preserved in the* Gospel of Thomas.

Into this dialogue are inserted the following sources: (1) a creation myth (127.23–131.15) based on Genesis 1–2; (2) a cosmological list (133.16–134.24) interpreted in the wisdom tradition; and (3) a fragment of an apocalyptic vision (134.24–137.3). The final redactor has introduced the entire document with (4) an exhortation, prayer, and typically gnostic instruction about the passage of the soul through

*the heavens (120.2–124.22), all of which is described in terms closely
related to the language of the deutero-Pauline corpus, upon which this
introductory section may well be dependent.*

The hand of the final redactor can also be detected throughout the
Dialogue of the Savior, *especially in his imposing a particular format
on the arrangement of the sources. The intent of the* Dialogue of the
Savior *appears to correspond to the first saying of the* Gospel of
Thomas: *to find the interpretation of Jesus' sayings in order not to
experience death. To attain this, the* Dialogue of the Savior *seems to be
arranged thematically to conform to an order of salvation like that
given in the second saying of the* Gospel of Thomas: *seeking-finding-
marveling-ruling-resting. In continuity with the dialogue source, the*
Dialogue of the Savior *develops this order of salvation to address one
main theological concern: eschatology. By an orderly arrangement of
the sources, eschatology is understood to be, paradoxically, both
available in the present and still awaited in the future: realized
eschatology is juxtaposed with futuristic eschatology. It is possible that
the entire document in its final form offers an elaborate interpretation
of baptism as the process that involves one's passing through death
("dissolution") and entering the "place of life."*

The Dialogue of the Savior *is an important witness to the history of
sayings traditions. Its use of sayings to compose dialogues marks a stage
in the development of the tradition leading from the primitive collection
of sayings to the creation of longer revelation discourses and dialogues.
In this respect, the* Dialogue of the Savior *is a precursor of the* Gospel of
John, *which much more subtly incorporates originally discrete sayings
into elaborate discourses and dialogues of Jesus. Moreover, in the
theological concern addressed by juxtaposing realized eschatology with
futuristic eschatology, the* Dialogue of the Savior *is also a harbinger of
the later redaction of* John. *Each document presents Jesus as a wisdom
teacher and living revealer, who challenges his disciples to discover how
revelation can come to be a reality within a community of believers.
Whereas the dialogue source probably dates from the second half of the
first century, the document in its final form was probably composed in
the mid- to late second century, when the deutero-Pauline corpus was
used in conjunction with gospel traditions to authenticate the interpretations of both the "orthodox" and the "heretics."*

*The text is divided according to the page and line numbers (120.1–
147.23) of the Coptic manuscript. The translation was made by Harold
W. Attridge* (The Nag Hammadi Library).

The Dialogue of the Savior

The Dialogue of the Savior

The Savior said to his disciples, "Already the time has come,
brothers, that we should leave behind [5] our labor and stand in the rest;
for he who stands in the rest will rest forever. And I say to you (pl.),
dwell in [10] heaven always [. . .] time [. . . . And I say] to you, [that
. . .] are afraid [. . .] to you. I [say to you], [15] the wrath is fearful, [and
he who] sets the wrath in motion is a man [. . .]. But since you have
[. . . when] they came from [. . .] they received these words [about it
(fem.)] with fear [20] and trembling. And it (fem.) made them stand with
archons, for from it (fem.) nothing came forth. But when I came, I
opened the way; I taught them [25] the passage through which will pass
the elect and the solitary ones 121 who have [learned of the Father],
since they have believed the truth.

"And as for all the glories that you give when you give glory, give
them in this way: [5] 'Hear us, Father, just as thou hast heard thine only-
begotten Son and hast taken him to thyself (and) given him rest from
many [labors. Thou] art he whose power [10] [is great, and] thy weapons
are [. . .] light [. . .] living [. . . who] cannot be touched [. . .] the
word of [15] [. . .] repentance of life [. . . from] thee. Thou art [the]
remembrance and all the serenity of the solitary ones. Again hear us,
just as thou hast heard [20] thine elect ones. These by thy sacrifice enter
in with their good deeds, they who have redeemed their souls from
these blind limbs in order that they might exist 122 forever. Amen.'

"I will teach you: When the time of the dissolution will come, the
first power of the darkness will [5] come upon you. Do not be afraid and
say, 'Behold the time has come.' But whenever you see a single staff in
the sky, that which (or: he who) [. . .] [10] not [. . .] [12] know that [. . .]
from the deed [. . .] and the archons [. . .] [15] come upon you [. . .].
Truly, fear is the power [of darkness]. If, then, you fear him who will
come upon you, that one will swallow you, [20] since there is not one
among them who will spare you or will have pity on you. But in this
way look at the [. . .] within him, since you have overcome every word
that is upon the earth. He 123 [will] take you up to the mountain
[where] there is no ruling authority [nor] tyrant. When you [come to it]
you will see the things that [5] [. . .]. And moreover [. . .] tell you that

[. . .] the reasoning power [. . .] reasoning power that exists [. . .] the
place of truth [10] [. . .] not, but they [. . .]. But you [. . .] of the truth,
that [which . . .] living mind because of [. . .] and your joy [15] [. . .]
you, in order that [. . .] your souls [. . .] lest he [. . .] the word [. . .]
which they lift up [20] [. . . and] they could not [. . .] which is [. . .].
The [. . .] did it [. . .]. For the crossing-place 124 is frightful before
[them]. But as for you, [with] single mind pass [it] by, for its depth is
great [and its] [5] height [is] exceedingly great. [. . .] single mind [. . .]
and the fire which [. . .] is. The lions [enclose . . .] all the powers
[. . .] [10] you; they will [. . .] and the powers [. . .] they [. . .]
beginning. I create [. . .] the soul from [. . .] [15] become a [. . .] in
every one [. . .] you are [. . .] and because [. . .] forget not [. . .] [20]
the sons of [. . .] and as you [. . .] you [. . .]."

Matthew said, "[In] what way [. . .]?" 125

The Savior said, " [. . .] those things that are in you (sing.) [. . .]
will remain, as for you, [. . .]."

Judas [said], "O Lord, [5] [. . .] the deeds [. . .] these souls, those
[which . . .] these little ones, when [. . .] where will they be? [. . .]
not, for the spirit [10] [. . .]."

The Lord [said, ". . .] [12] receive them; these do not die [nor] do they
perish, for they knew [15] [their] consorts and him who will take [them]
to himself. For truth seeks [after] the wise and the righteous one." The
Savior said, "The lamp [of the] body is the mind; as long as [20] you
(sing.) are upright [of heart]—which is [. . .]—then your (pl.) bodies
are [lights]. As long as your mind is [darkness], your light which you
126 wait for [will not be]. As for myself, I have called [. . .] that I shall
go [because . . .] my word to [him for whom] [5] I send."

His disciples [said, "Lord], who is the one who seeks [and who is the
one who] reveals?"

[The Lord said], "The one who seeks [is also the one who] [10]
reveals."

Matthew [said, "Lord], when I [. . .] what I said, who is the one
who [speaks and who] is the one who hears?"

[The Lord] said, [15] "The one who speaks is also the one who [hears],
and the one who sees [is] also the one who reveals."

Mariam said, "O Lord, behold, when I am bearing the body, [for
what reason do I] [20] weep, and for what reason do [I laugh]?"

The Lord said, "[If you (sing.)] weep because of its deeds [you will]
abide, and the mind laughs [. . .] 127 spirit. If one does not [. . . the]
darkness, he will [not] be able to see [the light]. Therefore [I] tell you
(pl.), [. . . of the] light is the darkness. [5] [And if one does not] stand in

[the darkness, he will not be able] to see the light. [. . .] the lie [. . .] were carried away by [. . .] you will give [. . .] and [10] [. . .] be for ever [. . .] in the [. . .] one [. . .] for ever. Then will [all] the powers [. . .] you, [15] those that are above and those [that] are below, in that place where [there will] be the weeping and [the gnashing] of teeth at the end of [all] these things."

Judas said, "Tell [20] [us], Lord, before [the heaven and] the earth were, what was it that [existed]?"

The Lord said, "It was darkness and water and 128 a spirit that was upon a [water]. But I say to [you, as for what] you seek after [and] inquire about, [behold, it is] [5] within you, and [. . .] of the power and the [mystery . . .] spirit, because from [. . .] the wickedness comes [. . .] the mind and [. . .] [10] behold [. . .] of the [. . .]."

[. . .] said, "Lord, tell us where [the soul (?)] stands, and where the true [mind (?)] [15] is?"

The Lord said [to him], "As for the fire [of the] spirit, it was in their [. . .]; therefore the [. . .] came to be. The true mind came to be [within] [20] them. [If] a man [establishes his soul (?)] in the height, then [he will] be exalted."

But Matthew asked [him about 129 . . .] that [. . .] received [. . .] he is the one who [. . .].

The Lord [said], "[. . .] steadfast against your [5] [. . .] outside you [. . .] him to set it [upon] you, and all things [. . .] your hearts. For just as your hearts [. . .] it, [10] so you will prevail over the powers that are [above] and those that are below. [But I] say to you, [he who is] able, let him deny [himself, and] repent. And he who [knows, [15] let him] seek and find and [rejoice]."

Judas said, "Behold, [. . .] see that everything is [in it] like these signs that are over [the earth]. For this reason they came to be like this (?)." [20]

The Lord [said], "When the Father [established] the world he [gathered] water from it. [His] Word came forth from him. 130 He dwelt in many [. . .]; he was more exalted than the path [of the sun that surrounds (?)] the whole earth. They (?) [. . .] for the water that was gathered [together] [5] was outside them. [. . .] of the water while a great fire [surrounded] them like walls. And [. . .] time, when many things were separating from [the] interior, when the [Father] [10] stood up, he looked [at the Word (?)] (and) said to him, 'Go, and [cast them] from you, in order that [the earth might not] be in want from generation to [generation] and from age to age.' Then [he] [15] cast forth from himself [springs] of milk, and springs [of] honey, and oil, and

[wine], and good fruits, and a sweet taste, and [20] good roots, [in order that] it might not be in want from generation [to] generation and from age [to] age. But he is above [. . .] **131** able to stand [. . .] his beauty [. . .] the deed. And outside of [. . .] is [. . .] of light, being able to [5] [. . .] the one who is like him, for he seizes upon the aeons that are [above] and that are below, [and they] took out of the fire [. . .]. It was scattered out of the [10] [Pleroma] that is above and [that is] below. As for everything that depends on them, they are [the things which exist] in heaven above [and on] earth below. [15] On them all things depend."

[And] when Judas heard these things he fell down, [worshipped], (and) gave glory to the Lord. Mariam asked, "Brothers, [20] [the things] about which you ask the Son of [. . .], where will you keep them?"

The Lord [said] to her, "Sister, [. . .] can seek out these things [. . .], since he has a place **132** to keep them in his heart [. . .] him to go from [. . .] and enter into [the place of life (?)] in order that he might not be confined [in] [5] this impoverished world."

Matthew said, "Lord, I wish [to see] that place of life, [that place] in which there is no evil, but rather it is [the] pure light."

The Lord said, [10] "Brother Matthew, you (sing.) cannot see it, as long as you wear the flesh."

Matthew said, "O Lord, even if [I can] not see it, let me [know it]." [15]

The Lord said, "Every one [of you] who has known himself has seen it; everything that is fitting for him to do, [he does] it. And he has been [doing] it in his goodness."

Judas [20] answered him and said, "Tell me, Lord, [the earthquake] that moves the earth, how does it move?"

The Lord took a stone [and] held it in his hand. [He **133** said, "What] is this that I hold in my [hand]?"

He said, "[It is] a stone."

He said to them, "He who sustains [the earth] is he who sustains the heaven. [5] When a word comes forth from the Greatness, it will go to him who sustains the heaven and the earth. For the earth does not move; if it moved, it would fall, but (it does not fall) in order that the first word [10] might not be annulled, namely 'he is the one who established the world, and he dwelt in it, and he received incense from it.' For everything that does not move I [will bring] to you, all ye sons of men, [15] for you are from [that] place.

"As for those who speak out of [joy] and truth, you are in their heart. And if he comes from [the] body of the Father through men, [20] [and] they do not receive him, [he] turns again to his place. He who knows

[not] the works of perfection knows nothing. If one does not stand in the darkness, he will not be able to see the light. 134 If one does not [understand] how the fire came to be, he will burn in it, because he does not know his root. 5 If one does not first understand the water, he does not know anything. For what is the use for him to receive baptism in it? If one does not understand how the wind that blows 10 came to be, he will run with it. If one does not understand how the body that he wears came to be, he will perish with it. And he who does not know the Son, 15 how will he know the [Father]? And he who will not know the root of all things, they (all things) are hidden from him. He who will not know the root of wickedness is not a stranger to it. He 20 who will not understand how he came will not understand how he will go, and is not a [stranger] to this world which [will perish and] which will be humbled."

Then he [took] Judas 25 and Matthew and Mariam 135 [. . . at] the end, the whole of heaven [and] earth. [And] when he set his [hand] upon them they hoped that they might [see] it. Judas lifted up his eyes; 5 he saw a very high place, and he saw the place of the pit, which is below.

Judas said to Matthew, "Brother, who can go up to this height or below 10 to the pit? For there is a great fire there, and a great terror." At that moment there came forth from it a word. While he was standing he saw how it came 15 [down]. Then he said to it, "Why have you (sing.) come down?"

And the Son of Man greeted them, and said to them, "A grain from a power was deficient and went down below to 20 [the] pit of the earth. And the greatness remembered, and sent the word to it. He brought it up to [his presence], because 136 the first word was abrogated."

[Again his] disciples wondered at all the [things] that he told them, they received them in faith, and they knew that it was not necessary [. . .] 5 to look at wickedness. Then he said [to] his disciples, "Did I not say to you (pl.) that just as sound and lightning are seen, so the good will be taken up to 10 the light?"

Then all his disciples gave glory to him. They said, "Lord, before you (sing.) appeared here, who was there to give glory to you? For through you are all glories. 15 And who was there to bless [you], since from you comes all blessing?"

While they were standing, he saw two spirits bringing a single soul with them in a great flash of lightning. 20 And a word came from the Son of Man, saying, "Give them their garment." [And] the little one was like the big one. They were [. . .] to (or: of) those who had received [them. 137 The disciples said to] each other, "Then we [. . . his] disciples, those whom he [. . .]."

Mariam [said, ". . .] see the ⁵ evil one [. . .] them from the beginning [. . .]."

The Lord said [to her], "When you see them [. . .] is great, they will not [. . .]. But when you ¹⁰ see Him Who Is Forever, that is the great vision."

Then all said to him, "Show it to us."

He said to them, "How do you wish to see it? [In] a vision which will cease? Or in an eternal vision?" ¹⁵ Again he said, "Strive to save the one [who] is able to follow [you]. Seek him and speak with him, in order that ²⁰ everyone whom you seek [may] agree with you. For I [say] to you, truly the living God [dwells] in you 138 [and you dwell (?)] in him."

Judas [said to him, "Truly] I wish [to . . .]."

The Lord [said] to him, "[The] living [God (?)], ⁵ since he exists, the entire [. . .] of the deficiency."

Judas [said], "Who will [rule over us (?)]?"

The Lord said, "[. . .] all the things that exist [. . .] the remainder, ¹⁰ it is they over which you [rule]."

Judas said, "Behold, the archons dwell in heaven; surely, then, it is they who will rule over us."

The Lord said, "You ¹⁵ will rule over them. But when you remove envy from you, then you will clothe yourselves with the light and enter into the bridal ²⁰ chamber."

Judas said, "How will our garments be brought to us?"

The Lord said, "Some will bring (them) to you [and] others will receive [them], 139 for they are [the ones who bring] you your garments. Who [can] reach that place which is the reward? But they gave the garments of life to ⁵ the man, for he knows the way on which he will go. For indeed it is a burden to me as well to reach it."

Mariam said, "Thus about 'The wickedness of each day,' and 'The ¹⁰ laborer being worthy of his food,' and 'The disciple resembling his teacher.' " This word she spoke as a woman who knew the All.

The disciples said to him, "What is the Pleroma and ¹⁵ what is the deficiency?"

He said to them, "You are from the Pleroma, and you dwell in the place where the deficiency is. And behold, its light was poured down ²⁰ upon me."

Matthew said, "Tell me, Lord, how the dead die, and how the living live?" 140

The Lord said, "[You (sing.) have] asked me for a word [about that] which eye has not seen, nor have I heard about it, except from you. But I say ⁵ to you (pl.), that when that which moves man is withdrawn he will be called 'dead,' and when the living one sets free the dead one, he will be called 'living.' "

Judas said, ¹⁰ "Why then, by the truth, do they die and live?"

The Lord said, "He who is from the truth does not die; he who is from the woman dies."

Mariam said, ¹⁵ "Tell me, Lord, why I have come to this place, to benefit or to suffer loss?"

The Lord said, "Because you (sing.) reveal the greatness of the revealer."

Mariam said to him, ²⁰ "Lord, is there then a place that is [. . .] or is deprived of the truth?"

The Lord said, "The place where I [am] not."

Mariam said, "Lord, you (sing.) are fearful and wonderful 141 and [. . .] from those who do not know [you]."

Matthew said, "Why do we not put ourselves to rest at once?" ⁵

The Lord said, "(You will) when you lay down these burdens."

Matthew said, "In what way does the little one cleave to the great one?"

The Lord said, "When you leave behind you ¹⁰ the things that will not be able to follow you, then you will put yourselves to rest."

Mariam said, "I want to know how all things exist."

The Lord said, ¹⁵ "Whoever seeks life (knows this), for [this] is their wealth. For the [enjoyment] of this world is a [lie], and its gold and its silver is error."

His disciples said to him, ²⁰ "What shall we do in order [that] our work may be perfect?"

The Lord [said] to them, "Be prepared before the All. Blessed is the man who has found 142 the interpretation [about this thought (?)], the struggle with his eyes. He did not kill nor was [he] killed, but he came forth victorious."

Judas said, "Tell me, Lord, ⁵ what is the beginning of the way?"

He said, "Love and goodness. For if there had been one of these dwelling with the archons, wickedness would never have come to be."

Matthew said, "O Lord, ¹⁰ you (sing.) have spoken without pain of the end of the All."

The Lord said, "Everything which I have said to you (pl.) you have understood and received in faith. If you have known them, they are [yours]; ¹⁵ if not, they are not yours."

They said to him, "What is the place to which we shall go?"

The Lord said, "The place which you can reach, stand there!" [20]

Mariam said, "Is everything [that] is established seen in this way?"

The Lord said, "I have told you (pl.) [that] he who sees is he who reveals."

His twelve disciples asked him, [25] "Teacher, 143 as for the lack of care [. . .] teach us that [. . .]."

The Lord said, "[If you understood] everything which I said [to you, then] you will [5] [. . .], you [will know] everything."

Mariam said, "There is one word that I will [say] to the Lord concerning the mystery of the truth, this in which we have stood. Moreover, [10] it is to the worldly that we appear."

Judas said to Matthew, "We wish to know with what kind [of] garments we will be clothed, when we come forth from the corruption of the [15] [flesh]."

The Lord said, "The archons [and] the governors have garments that are given to them for a time, which do not abide. As for you, [however], since you are sons of the truth, it is not [20] with these temporary garments that you will clothe yourselves. Rather, I say to you that you will be blessed when you strip yourselves, for it is still a great thing 144 [. . .] outside."

[. . .] said, " [. . . the] word, I am [. . .]."

The Lord said, " [. . .] your father [5] [. . .]."

Mariam said, "[What] is this mustard [seed] like? [Is it] from heaven [or] from [the] earth?"

The Lord said, "When [the] Father established the [10] world for himself, he left behind many things from the Mother of the All. Because of this he speaks and acts."

Judas said, "You (sing.) have said this [to] us from the mind of truth. When we pray, [15] how should we pray?"

The Lord said, "Pray in the place where there is no woman."

Matthew said, "He says to us, 'Pray in the place where there is [no] woman,' (and) 'Destroy [the] [20] works of femaleness,' not because she is another [. . .], but so that they (the works) will cease [from you]."

Mariam said, "Will they never be destroyed?"

The Lord said, "[. . .] is the one who knows that [the works] of [femaleness] will dissolve 145 and be [destroyed (?)] . . . in this] place."

Judas said to Matthew, "The works of [5] femaleness will dissolve [. . .] the archons [. . .] will be [. . .] is [. . .] they see you [. . .] receive [10] [. . .] a word [. . .] the Father [. . .] and a lightning [. . .] or they [. . .] more [15] [. . .] honor [. . .] authority [. . . the] Father and the Son [. . .] one of [. . .] to walk in [. . .] [21] be great [. . .] I [. . .] burden [. . .]." 146

[The Lord] said [to them], "When [. . .] the works that dissolve [. . .] a work [. . .] who [5] know [. . .] dissolve [. . .] his (or: its) place [. . .] while he [. . .]." The Lord said, " [. . .] [10] the [. . .] for in what he [. . .] light."

[. . .] said, " [. . .] in him [. . .] who is [. . . ? . . .] [15] of whom [from . . .] the world [. . .] the drink of oil [. . .]."

The Lord said, " [. . .] who has understood [. . .] [20] does the [. . .] [24] your [. . . 147 13] they] will mock [. . .] for I say [15] [. . .] take [. . .] you many [. . .] who sought, having [. . .] understand this [. . .] will live for [20] [ever]. But [I myself] say to [you . . .] that you might not err [in your] spirits and your souls."

[The] Dialogue of the Savior

The Gospel of the Egyptians

The Gospel of the Egyptians (Gos. Eg.) *is composed of sayings that are attributed to Jesus and partially preserved in Greek in a few quotations in the writings of Clement of Alexandria (a church writer who lived at the end of the second century* C.E.*). This gospel was frequently referred to by name in the second and third centuries, and undoubtedly was widely used and well-respected in Egypt during that time. Unfortunately, there is no material evidence of the contents of the text apart from the brief citations by Clement. The designation, the* Gospel of the Egyptians, *suggests that this document was named after the land and its inhabitants, and may imply that this was the gospel used by at least one segment of the Egyptian Christian populace. This* Gospel of the Egyptians *is to be differentiated from another, completely different writing with the same name which is part of the Coptic Gnostic Library from Nag Hammadi.*

Despite the paucity of the extant fragments, the theology of the Gospel of the Egyptians *is clear: each fragment endorses sexual asceticism as the means of breaking the lethal cycle of birth and of overcoming the alleged sinful differences between male and female, enabling all persons to return to what was understood to be their primordial androgynous state. This theology is reflected in speculative interpretations of the Genesis accounts of the Creation and the Fall (Gen. 1:27; 2:16–17, 24; 3:21), according to which the unity of the first man was disrupted by the creation of woman and sexual division. Salvation was thus thought to be the recapitulation of Adam and Eve's primordial state, the removal of the body and the reunion of the sexes. This return to the primordial state was said to be accomplished—or at least symbolized—by baptism. In this respect, the* Gospel of the Egyptians *is to be compared with Paul's Letters to the Galatians (Gal.*

3:26–28) and the Corinthians (I Cor. 12:13), which presuppose this baptismal theology but use the tradition differently, interpreting the theme of unity as a social category to refer to the unity of Jews and Greeks, slaves and freedmen, males and females.

In the Gospel of the Egyptians, this ascetic theology is included among the traditions of sayings of Jesus. Here, too, comparison should be made with Paul's first Letter to the Corinthians, where appeals to sayings traditions were made both by Paul and by the "enthusiasts" with whom he contended (I Cor. 1–4; 7). The Gospel of Luke (Luke 17:26–30; 20:34–36) also reinterpreted traditional sayings to encourage celibacy. Many of the sayings in the Gospel of the Egyptians, moreover, have been used to compose brief dialogues between Jesus and Salome. This compositional technique parallels that of some of the sayings in the Gospel of Thomas and a number of those in the Dialogue of the Savior, both in terms of form and structure and in terms of subject matter and content. The most original form of the baptismal tradition, in fact, is that preserved in the Gospel of the Egyptians, where it is regarded as a saying of Jesus given in response to a question of Salome. This tradition is also found as a free-floating saying three times in the Gospel of Thomas, once in an anonymous early Christian homily known as 2 Clement, and in several non-canonical apostolic Acts. Vestiges also underlie some of the sayings in the earliest source of the Dialogue of the Savior and, perhaps, the Gospel of John (John 11:25) as well.

If an Egyptian provenance is granted, the Gospel of the Egyptians shows that the Jesus movement there was, from the outset, influenced by gnosticism. It demonstrates, moreover, the orientation of this particular Egyptian community toward traditions of sayings of Jesus rather than toward the more speculative, systematic writings of other gnostic groups. The earliest possible date for the composition of this gospel would be in the middle of the first century, when sayings traditions such as those attested in I Corinthians were being circulated. The latest possible date would be in the middle of the second century, when certain gnostic groups appropriated this gospel, making use of these sayings which shortly thereafter were quoted by Clement. Based on compositional parallels in the morphology of the tradition, a date in the late first or early second century is most likely.

In the gospel citations that follow, care should be taken to distinguish between the actual quotations of the text of the Gospel of the Egyptians and Clement's own interpretive comments.

The text is listed by the number of the preserved fragments (1–6). The *translation was made by Wilhelm Schneemelcher and George Ogg* (New Testament Apocrypha).

The Gospel of the Egyptians

1. When Salome asked, "How long will death have power?" the Lord answered, "So long as ye women bear children"—not as if life was something bad and creation evil, but as teaching the sequence of nature.

   (Clement, *Stromateis* 3.6.45.3)

2. Those who are opposed to God's creation because of continence, which has a fair-sounding name, also quote the words addressed to Salome which I mentioned earlier. They are handed down, as I believe, in the Gospel of the Egyptians. For, they say: the Savior himself said, "I am come to undo the works of the female," by the female meaning lust, and by the works birth and decay.

   (Ibid., 3.9.63.1–2)

3. Since then the Word has alluded to the consummation, Salome saith rightly, "Until when shall men die?" Now Scripture uses the term 'man' in the two senses, of the visible outward form and of the soul, and again of the redeemed man and of him who is not redeemed. And sin is called the death of the soul. Wherefore the Lord answers advisedly, "So long as women bear children," i.e., so long as lusts are powerful.

   (Ibid., 3.9.64.1)

4. Why do they not also adduce what follows the words spoken to Salome, these people who do anything but walk by the gospel rule according to truth? For when she said, "I have then done well in not bearing children," as if it were improper to engage in procreation, then the Lord answered and said, "Eat every plant, but that which has bitterness eat not."

   (Ibid., 3.9.66.1–2)

5. Contending further for the impious doctrine he (Julius Cassianus) adds: "And how could a charge not be rightly brought against the

Savior, if he has transformed us and freed us from error, and delivered us from sexual intercourse?" In this matter his teaching is similar to that of Tatian. But he emerged from the school of Valentinus. Therefore Cassianus now says, When Salome asked when what she had inquired about would be known, the Lord said, "When you have trampled on the garment of shame and when the two become one and the male with the female (is) neither male nor female." Now in the first place we have not this word in the four Gospels that have been handed down to us, but in the Gospel of the Egyptians. Further he seems to me to fail to recognize that by the male impulse is meant wrath and by the female lust.

(Ibid., 3.13.92.1–93.1)

6. And when the Savior says to Salome that death will reign as long as women bear children, he does not thereby slander procreation, for that indeed is necessary for the redemption of believers.

(Clement, *Excerpta ex Theodoto* 67.2)

Papyrus Oxyrhynchus 840

Papyrus Oxyrhynchus 840 (Pap. Oxy. 840) *is a single leaf of a miniature Greek parchment codex (measuring 8.8 × 7.4 cm) that contains the conclusion of a discourse between Jesus and his disciples and the greater part of a controversy story between Jesus and a Pharisaic chief priest in the Temple at Jerusalem. Discovered in Egypt in 1905, and immediately designated the "Fragment of an Uncanonical Gospel," the codex from which this leaf comes was possibly worn around the neck as an amulet. The codex has been assigned a date in the fourth or, less likely, the fifth century* C.E.*, but the lost original, of which this is a copy, is much earlier.* Papyrus Oxyrhynchus 840 *is conserved today in the Bodleian Library, Oxford University.*

The controversy story, which makes up most of the extant text, originally circulated in oral form. It exhibits close parallels with the form, literary style, and content of Mark 7:1–23 and parallels. The discussion of Jewish rites of purification in connection with Temple worship points to a milieu in which believers in Jesus were beginning to define themselves in relation to emerging Pharisaic Judaism. The ascription of such a controversy to the life of Jesus, moreover, serves to situate the debate in the past, with Jesus himself, and to secure the authority of Jesus over against that of the Pharisees. Thus, it is probable that this story was put into written form in the second half of the first century C.E.*, most likely in Syria. The use of the term "Savior" as a title for Jesus is distinctive, inasmuch as it is unattested elsewhere in gospel traditions which purport to describe events in the life of Jesus.*

The text is divided according to the reverse and front sides of the Greek manuscript. The translation was made by Joachim Jeremias and George Ogg (New Testament Apocrypha).

Papyrus Oxyrhynchus 840

Verso First before he does wrong (?) he thinks out everything that is crafty. But be ye on your guard that the same thing may not happen to you as does to them. For not only among the living do evil doers among men receive retribution, but they must also suffer punishment and great torment.

And he took them (the disciples) with him into the place of purification itself and walked about in the Temple court. And a Pharisaic chief priest, Levi (?) by name, fell in with them and s[aid] to the Savior: Who gave thee leave to [trea]d this place of purification and to look upon [the]se holy utensils without having bathed thyself and even without thy disciples having [wa]shed their f[eet]? On the contrary, being defi[led], thou hast trodden the Temple court, this clean p[lace], although no [one who] has [not] first bathed himself or [chang]ed his clot[hes] may tread it and [venture] to vi[ew these] holy utensils! Forthwith [the Savior] s[tood] still with h[is] disciples and [answered]: **Recto** How stands it (then) with thee, thou art forsooth (also) here in the Temple court. Art thou then clean? He said to him: I am clean. For I have bathed myself in the pool of David and have gone down by the one stair and come up by the other and have put on white and clean clothes, and (only) then have I come hither and have viewed these holy utensils. Then said the Savior to him: Woe unto you blind that see not! Thou hast bathed thyself in water that is poured out, in which dogs and swine lie night and day and thou hast washed thyself and hast chafed thine outer skin, which prostitutes also and flute-girls anoint, bathe, chafe and rouge, in order to arouse desire in men, but within they are full of scorpions and of [bad]ness [of every kind]. But I and [my disciples], of whom thou sayest that we have not im[mersed] ourselves, [have been im]mersed in the liv[ing . . .] water which comes down from [. . . B]ut woe unto them that . . .

The Apocryphon of James

The Apocryphon of James (Ap. Jas.) *is a Coptic translation of an originally Greek document that gives an account of the teachings of Jesus in the form of a dialogue between Jesus and two of his disciples, Peter and James. Since the document was untitled in the original, scholars have assigned its title on the basis of the document's own reference to itself as a "secret book" (Greek:* apocryphon) *which allegedly was revealed by Jesus to his brother, James the Just. The* Apocryphon of James *is the second of five tractates of Codex I of the Coptic Gnostic Library, which was buried in the fourth century and discovered in Egypt in 1945. This Codex is commonly known as the Jung Codex, after the name of the Jung Institute in Zurich, which acquired the text in 1952. When first published in 1968, the document was referred to as the* Epistula Iacobi Apocrypha. *Today it is housed in the Coptic Museum of Old Cairo.*

Unlike the four gospels that came to be included in the New Testament, the body of the Apocryphon of James *has no narrative structure. Instead, it preserves sayings, prophecies, parables, and rules for the community which are attributed to Jesus, secondarily inserted into an account of a post-resurrection appearance, and, in turn, embedded into the frame of a letter, allegedly written in Hebrew by James, for the instruction and edification of an unidentified group of Christians. In the first half of the* Apocryphon of James, *sayings are used as the basis of a dialogue between Jesus and his disciples, Peter and James. The use of dialogue is almost completely absent from the discourse of the second half, and, indeed, seems to be a secondary literary technique used throughout the entire document.*

The identification of the sources of the traditions used in the Apocryphon of James *is a matter of considerable debate. The epistolary*

frame which serves to introduce the document, however, provides a clue
to the use of sources and to the date and nature of composition. The
opening paragraphs of the Apocryphon of James describe a situation in
which scribal activity was taking place. The disciples of Jesus were
gathered together after Jesus' resurrection and, remembering what Jesus
had said to each one of them, were setting it down in books. This scene
suggests that this took place at a time when the literary production of
sayings of Jesus was still being vigorously pursued, a time in which
written texts with "scriptural" authority were not yet normative.
Moreover, only some of the sayings that are in the Apocryphon of James
are also found in the New Testament. Analysis of each of these sayings
provides no evidence that the Apocryphon of James either knew of or is
literarily dependent upon any of the writings of the New Testament.
Most of all, appeals to particular disciples or apostles of Jesus as
authorities for local communities were well known in the second, third,
and fourth generations of Christianity. The appeal to James suggests
that the Apocryphon of James dates from a time when written
traditions about Jesus were connected with the competitive claims of
authority under the names of individual disciples of Jesus.

All of this implies that the Apocryphon of James is an early
Christian writing based on an independent sayings collection that was
contemporary with other early Christian writings which presented
sayings of Jesus. The earliest possible date of composition would be
sometime in the first century; the latest possible date would be at the
end of the second or the beginning of the third century, when the gospels
of the New Testament began to be known, read, and used as
authoritative texts in the struggle against the "heretics." The freedom in
the use of sayings and the role of Peter and James as authority figures in
the transmission of the tradition suggest that the Apocryphon of James
was probably composed in the first half of the second century. Internal
evidence intimates that Egypt was its place of origin. The use of
individually discrete sayings of Jesus in the composition of discourses
and dialogues makes it an important witness to the use and development of sayings traditions. In some instances, sayings that are
transmitted as words of Jesus in the synoptic gospels are, in the
Apocryphon of James, preserved as questions or comments of the
disciples. The Apocryphon of James can thus be profitably compared
with the Gospel of John, which also uses individual sayings to compose
Jesus' dialogues in the first half of the gospel as well as his "farewell
discourse" in the second half.

The text is divided according to the page and line numbers (1.1– 16.30) of the Coptic manuscript. The translation was made by the editor, Ron Cameron.

The Apocryphon of James

1 [James writes] to [. . .]. Peace [be with you (sing.) from] Peace, [love from] Love, ⁵ [grace from] Grace, [faith] from Faith, life from Holy Life!

Since you (sing.) asked me to send ¹⁰ you a secret book <which> was revealed to me and Peter by the Lord, I could neither refuse you nor speak (directly) to you, ¹⁵ but [I have written] it in Hebrew letters and have sent it to you—and to you alone. But inasmuch as you are a minister of the salvation ²⁰ of the saints, endeavor earnestly and take care not to recount this book to many—this which the Savior did not desire [to] recount to all of us, his ²⁵ twelve disciples. But blessed are those who will be saved through faith in this discourse.

Now I sent you ³⁰ ten months ago another secret book which the Savior revealed to me. But that one you are to regard in this manner, as revealed ³⁵ to me, James. And this one, 2 [. . . revealed . . .] those who [. . .], therefore, and seek [. . .] ⁵ thus also [. . .] salvation and [. . .].

Now the twelve disciples [were] sitting all together at [the same time], ¹⁰ and, remembering what the Savior had said to each one of them, whether secretly or openly, they were setting it down ¹⁵ in books. [And] I was writing what was in [my book]—lo, the Savior appeared, [after] he had departed from [us while we] gazed at him. And five hundred and fifty ²⁰ days after he arose from the dead, we said to him: "Have you gone and departed from us?"

And Jesus said: "No, but I shall go to the place from which I have come. ²⁵ If you (pl.) desire to come with me, come."

They all answered and said: "If you bid us, we'll come."

He said: "Truly I say to you (pl.), ³⁰ no one ever will enter the Kingdom of Heaven if I bid him, but rather because you yourselves are full. Let me have James and Peter, ³⁵ in order that I may fill them."

And when he called these two, he took them aside, and commanded the rest to busy themselves with that with which they had been busy.

⁴⁰ The Savior said: "You (pl.) have received mercy **3** [. . .] become [. . .] they wrote [. . .] book, as [. . .] to you again [. . .] ⁵ and just as [. . .] they [. . .] hear and [. . .] they [. . .] understand. Do you not desire, then, to be filled? And is your heart <drunk>? ¹⁰ Do you not desire, then, to be sober? Therefore, be ashamed! And now, waking or sleeping, remember that you have seen the Son of Man, and with him ¹⁵ you have spoken, and to him you have listened. Woe to those who have seen the Son [of] Man! Blessed are those (or: you [pl.]) ²⁰ who have not seen the Man, and who have not consorted with him, and who have not spoken with him, and who have not listened to anything from him. Yours is ²⁵ life! Know, therefore, that he healed you when you were ill, in order that you might reign. Woe to those who have rested from their illness, because they will ³⁰ relapse again into illness! Blessed are those (or: you [pl.]) who have not been ill, and have known rest before they (or: you) became ill. Yours is the Kingdom of God! Therefore I ³⁵ say to you, become full and leave no place within you empty, since the Coming One is able to mock you."

Then Peter answered: "<Lord>, three ⁴⁰ times you have said to us, **4** '[Become full,' but] we are full."

The [Lord answered and] said: "[Therefore I say] to you (pl.), [become full], in order that ⁵ [you] may not [be diminished. Those who are diminished], however, will not [be saved]. For fullness is good [and diminution] is bad. Therefore, just as it is good for you (sing.) to be diminished and, on the other hand, bad for you to be filled, so also ¹⁰ the one who is full is diminished; and the one who is diminished is not filled as the one who is diminished is filled, and the one who is full, for his part, brings his sufficiency to completion. Therefore, it is fitting to be diminished ¹⁵ while you (pl.) can (still) be filled, and to be filled while it is (still) possible to be diminished, in order that you can [fill] yourselves the more. Therefore, [become] full of the spirit ²⁰ but be diminished of reason. For reason is (of) the soul; and it is soul."

And I answered and said to him: "Lord, we can obey you ²⁵ if you wish. For we have forsaken our forefathers and our mothers and our villages and have followed you. Grant us, [therefore], ³⁰ not to be tempted by the wicked devil."

The Lord answered and said: "What is your (pl.) merit when you do the will of the Father if it is not given to you by him ³⁵ as a gift, while you are tempted by Satan? But if you are oppressed by Satan and are ⁴⁰ persecuted and you do his (i.e., the Father's) 5 will, I [say] that he will love you and will make you equal with me and will consider that you have become [5] [beloved] through his providence according to your free choice. Will you not cease, then, being lovers of the flesh and being afraid of sufferings? Or do [10] you not know that you have not yet been mistreated and have not yet been accused unjustly, nor have you yet been shut up in prison, nor [15] have you yet been condemned lawlessly, nor have you yet been crucified <without> reason, nor have you yet been buried <shamefully>, as (was) I myself, [20] by the evil one? Do you dare to spare the flesh, you for whom the spirit is an encircling wall? If you contemplate the world, how long it is [25] <before> you and also how long it is after you, you will find that your life is one single day and your sufferings, one single hour. For the good (pl.) [30] will not enter the world. Scorn death, therefore, and take concern for life. Remember my cross and my death and you will [35] live."

And I answered and said to him: "Lord, do not mention to us the cross and the death, for they are far 6 from you."

The Lord answered and said: "Truly I say to you (pl.), none will be saved unless they believe in my cross. [5] [But] those who have believed in my cross, theirs is the Kingdom of God. Therefore, become seekers for death, just as the dead who seek for life, [10] for that for which they seek is revealed to them. And what is there to concern them? When you turn yourselves towards death, it will make known to you election. In truth [15] I say to you, none of those who are afraid of death will be saved. For the Kingdom of <God> belongs to those who have put themselves to death. Become better than I; [20] make yourselves like the son of the Holy Spirit."

Then I questioned him: "Lord, how may we prophesy to those who ask us to prophesy [25] to them? For there are many who ask us and who look to us to hear an oracle from us."

The Lord answered and said: "Do you (pl.) [30] not know that the head of prophecy was cut off with John?"

And I said: "Lord, it is not possible to remove the head of prophecy, is it?"

The Lord said [35] to me: "When you (pl.) come to know what 'head' is, and that prophecy issues from the head, (then) understand what is (the meaning of) 'Its head was removed.' 7 I first spoke with you in parables, and you did not understand. Now, in turn, I speak with [5] you openly, and you do not perceive. But it is you who were to me a parable in parables and what is apparent [10] in what are open.

"Be zealous to be saved without being urged. Rather, be ready on your (pl.) own and, if possible, go before me. [15] For thus the Father will love you.

"Become haters of hypocrisy and evil thought. For it is thought [20] which gives birth to hypocrisy, but hypocrisy is far from the truth.

"Let not the Kingdom of Heaven wither away. For it is like a date-palm <shoot> [25] whose fruits poured down around it. It put forth leaves and, when they budded, they caused the productivity (of the date-palm) to dry up. Thus it is also with the fruit which [30] came from this single root: when it (i.e., the fruit) was <picked>, fruits were collected by many (harvesters). It would indeed be good if [35] it were possible to produce these new plants now; (for then) you (sing.) would find it (i.e., the Kingdom).

"<Since> I have been glorified in this manner before this time, why do you (pl.) restrain me when I am eager to go? 8 For after the [. . .] you have constrained me to remain with you eighteen more days (or: <months>) for the sake of the parables. It sufficed [5] for some persons <to> pay attention to the teaching and to understand 'The Shepherds' and 'The Seed' and 'The Building' and 'The Lamps of the Virgins' and 'The Wage of the Workers' and 'The Double Drachma' and 'The Woman.'

[10] "Become zealous about the Word. For the Word's first condition is faith; the second is love; the third is works. [15] Now from these comes life. For the Word is like a grain of wheat. When someone sowed it, he believed in it; and when it sprouted, he loved it, because he looked (forward to) [20] many grains in the place of one; and when he worked (it), he was saved, because he prepared it for food. Again he left (some grains) to sow. Thus it is also possible for you (pl.) to receive [25] the Kingdom of Heaven: unless you receive it through knowledge, you will not be able to find it.

"Therefore I say to you (pl.), be sober. Do not go astray. [30] And many times I have said to you all together—and also to you (sing.) alone, James, I have said—be saved. And I have commanded you (sing.) to follow me, [35] and I have taught you the response in the presence of the Rulers. Observe that I have descended, and I have spoken, and <I> have troubled myself, and I have received my crown, 9 when I saved you (pl.). For I have descended to dwell with you in order that <you> also may dwell with me. And [5] when I found that your houses had no ceilings over them, I dwelt in houses which would be able to receive me when I descended.

"Therefore, obey [10] me, my brothers. Understand what the great light is. The Father does not need me. For a father does not need a son, but it is the son who needs [15] the father. To him I am going, for the Father of the Son is not in need of you (pl.).

"Pay attention to the Word. Understand knowledge. Love life. [20] And no one will persecute you (pl.), nor will any one oppress you, other than you yourselves.

"O you (pl.) wretched! O you [25] unfortunates! O you dissemblers of the truth! O you falsifiers of knowledge! O you sinners against the spirit! Do you even now dare [30] to listen, when it behooved you to speak from the beginning? Do you even now dare to sleep, when it behooved you to be awake from the beginning, in order that [35] the Kingdom of Heaven might receive you? 10 In truth I say to you, it is easier for a holy one to sink into defilement, and for a man of light to sink into [5] darkness, than for you to reign—or (even) not to (reign)!

"I have remembered your (pl.) tears and your grief and your sorrow. They are far from us. Now, then, you who are [10] outside the inheritance of the Father, weep where it behooves (you) and grieve and proclaim that which is good, since the Son is ascending appropriately. [15] In truth I say to you, had it been to those who would listen to me that I was sent, and had it been with them that I was to speak, I would have never descended [20] upon the earth. And now, then, be ashamed on account of them.

"Behold, I shall depart from you (pl.). I am going and I do not desire to remain with you any longer—just as [25] you yourselves have not desired. Now, then, follow me quickly. Therefore I say to you, for your sake I have descended. You are [30] the beloved; you are those who will become a cause of life for many. Beseech the Father. Implore God often, and he will give to you. Blessed [35] is the one who has seen you with him when he is proclaimed among the angels and glorified among the saints. Yours is life! Rejoice and be glad as 11 children of God. Keep [his] will in order that you may be saved. Take reproof from me and save yourselves. I intercede [5] on your behalf with the Father, and he will forgive you much."

And when we heard these things, we became elated, for <we> had been depressed on account of what we had said earlier. [10] Now when he saw our rejoicing, he said: "Woe to you (pl.) who are in want of an advocate! Woe to you who are in need of grace! Blessed are [15] those who have spoken freely and have produced grace for themselves. Make yourselves like strangers; of what sort are they in the estimation of your

[20] city? Why are you troubled when you oust yourselves of your own accord and depart from your city? Why do you abandon your dwelling place [25] of your own accord, readying it for those who desire to dwell in it? O you exiles and fugitives! Woe to you, because you will be caught! Or [30] perhaps you imagine that the Father is a lover of humanity? Or that he is persuaded by prayers? Or that he is gracious to one on behalf of another? Or that he bears with one who seeks? [35] For he knows the desire and also that which the flesh needs. Because it is not it (i.e., the flesh) which yearns for the soul. For without the soul the body does not sin, just as [12] the soul is not saved without (the) spirit. But if the soul is saved (when it is) without evil, and if the spirit also is saved, (then) the body [5] becomes sinless. For it is the spirit which <animates> the soul, but it is the body which kills it—that is, it is it (i.e., the soul) which kills itself. Truly I say to you (pl.), [10] he (i.e., the Father) will not forgive the sin of the soul at all, nor the guilt of the flesh. For none of those who have worn the flesh will be saved. For do you imagine that many have found [15] the Kingdom of Heaven? Blessed is the one who has seen himself as a fourth one in heaven."

When we heard these things, we became distressed. Now when he saw that we were distressed, [20] he said: "This is why I say this to you (pl.), that you may know yourselves. For the Kingdom of Heaven is like an ear of grain which sprouted in a field. And [25] when it ripened, it scattered its fruit and, in turn, filled the field with ears of grain for another year. You also: be zealous to reap for yourselves an ear of life, in order that [30] you may be filled with the Kingdom.

"As long as I am with you (pl.), give heed to me and obey me. But when I am to depart from you, [35] remember me. And remember me because I was with you without your knowing me. Blessed are those who have known me. Woe to those who have [40] heard and have not believed! Blessed are those who [13] have not seen [but] have [had faith].

"And once again I [persuade] you (pl.). For I am revealed to you building a house which is very valuable [5] to you, since you take shelter under it; in the same way it will be able to support the house of your neighbors when (theirs) is in danger [of] falling. In truth I say to you, woe [10] to those on behalf of whom I was sent down to this place! Blessed are those who are to ascend to the Father. Again I reprove you. You who are, make yourselves like [15] those who are not, in order that you may come to be with those who are not.

"Let not the Kingdom of Heaven become desolate among you (pl.). Do not become arrogant [20] on account of the light which illumines. Rather, become to yourselves in this manner, as I (am) to you. For you

I have placed myself under the curse, in order that you [25] may be saved."

And Peter answered to this and said: "Sometimes you urge us on to the Kingdom of Heaven, [30] and other times you turn us away, Lord. Sometimes you persuade (us) and impel us to faith and promise us life, and other times you expel [35] us from the Kingdom of Heaven."

And the Lord answered and said to us: "I have given you (pl.) faith many times. Moreover, I have revealed myself to you (sing.), [14] James, and you (pl.) have not known me. Again, now I see you rejoicing many times. And when you are elated [5] over [the] promise of life, are you nevertheless glum? And are you distressed when you are taught about the Kingdom? But you through faith [and] knowledge have received [10] life. Therefore, scorn rejection when you hear it, but, when you hear the promise, be the more glad. In truth I say to you, [15] the one who will receive life and believe in the Kingdom will never leave it—not even if the Father desires to banish him!

"These things I shall say to [20] you (pl.) for the present. But now I shall ascend to the place from which I have come. But you, when I was eager to go, have driven me out, and, instead of your accompanying me, [25] you have pursued me. But give heed to the glory which awaits me, and, having opened your heart(s), listen to the hymns which await me up in heaven. [30] For today I am obliged to take (my place) at the right hand of my Father. Now I have said (my) last word to you. I shall part from you. For a chariot of wind has taken me up, [35] and from now on I shall strip myself in order that I may clothe myself. But give heed: blessed are those who have preached the Son before he descended, [40] in order that, when I have come, I (or: <they>) may ascend. Thrice blessed [15] are those who [were] proclaimed by the Son before they came into being, in order that you may have a portion with [5] them."

When he said these things, he went (away). And we knelt down, I and Peter, and gave thanks, and sent our heart(s) up to heaven. We heard with [10] our ears and saw with our eyes the sound of wars and a trumpet-call and a great commotion.

And when we passed beyond that place, [15] we sent our mind(s) up further. And we saw with our eyes and heard with our ears hymns and angelic praises and [20] angelic jubilation. And heavenly majesties were hymning, and we ourselves were jubilant.

After this, we also desired to send our [25] spirit(s) above to the Majesty. And when we ascended, we were permitted neither to see nor to hear anything. For the rest of the disciples called to us and [30]

questioned us: "What is it that you (pl.) have heard from the Master?"
And, "What has he said to you?" And, "Where has he gone?"

And we answered [35] them: "He has ascended." And, "He has given
us a pledge and has promised us all life and has disclosed to us children
who are to come after us, since he has bid 16 [us to] love them,
inasmuch as we will [be saved] for their sake."

And when they heard, they believed the revelation, but were angry
about [5] those who would be born. Then I, not desiring to entice them
to scandal, sent each one to another place. But I myself went up to
Jerusalem, praying that I may [10] obtain a portion with the beloved who
are to be revealed.

And I pray that the beginning may come from you (sing.), for thus I
can be saved. [15] Because they will be enlightened through me, through
my faith and through another's which is better than mine, for I desire
that mine become the lesser. [20] Endeavor earnestly, therefore, to make
yourself like them, and pray that you may obtain a portion with them.
For apart from what I have recounted, the Savior did not [25] disclose
revelation to us. For their sake we proclaim, indeed, a portion with
those for whom (it) was proclaimed, those whom the Lord has made
his [30] children.

TRADITIONS
OF STORIES
ABOUT JESUS

The Secret Gospel of Mark

The Secret Gospel of Mark (Secret Mark) *is a fragment of an early edition of the Gospel of Mark which contains an account of the raising of a young man from the dead, a rite of initiation, and a brief excerpt of an encounter between Jesus and three women. The* Secret Gospel of Mark *is preserved in Greek in a fragment of a letter of Clement of Alexandria (a church writer who lived at the end of the second century), in which he denounces the Carpocratians (a libertine group of Christian gnostics who were prominent throughout the second century). This fragment was discovered by Morton Smith in 1958 at the Monastery of Mar Saba, located roughly twelve miles southeast of Jerusalem in the Judean desert. On paleographical grounds the copy of the letter has been assigned a date in the second half of the eighteenth century, at which time it was copied into the back of a 1646 edition of letters of Ignatius of Antioch (a church writer who lived at the beginning of the second century).*

In his letter, Clement responds to certain questions he had received about the text of the Secret Gospel of Mark. *He presents the following schema of the various alleged editions of the Gospel of Mark: first, Mark wrote "an account of the Lord's doings" for catechumens, in which he selected what he thought was most suitable for beginners in the faith; second, Mark also wrote another, "more spiritual Gospel," to be used by those who were being perfected in the faith; and third, Mark knew of additional, arcane traditions—which he did not write down—which would lead initiates into the "innermost sanctuary" of the truth.*

The fragments of the Secret Gospel of Mark *are located between Mark 10:34 and 35 and after Mark 10:46a. In the first fragment, the account of the raising of the young man from the dead is a variant of the story of the raising of Lazarus in the Gospel of John (John 11). On form-*

critical and redaction-critical grounds, the version of the story in the Secret Gospel of Mark is to be judged more primitive than the one preserved in John 11. Immediately following this story is the report of the initiation of this young man. The technical term used to describe this rite, the "mystery of the kingdom of God," suggests that this nocturnal initiation most likely refers to baptism. The second fragment, which comes after Mark 10:46a, seems to be a remnant of an encounter between Jesus and this young initiate's family in Jericho.

The Secret Gospel of Mark is an important witness to the history and development of gospel traditions. The close similarity between the stories of the raisings from the dead in the Secret Gospel of Mark and in the Gospel of John suggests that Mark and John have drawn upon a shared tradition, and raises the question whether this story came from a common collection, perhaps written in Aramaic, from which Mark and John have also taken their other miracle stories. Moreover, since this story occurs in the same sequence in the structural outline of both the Secret Gospel of Mark and the Gospel of John, it is possible that this story is part of a more comprehensive source used independently by both evangelists.

Most of all, the discovery of the Secret Gospel of Mark has made us privy to new and unparalleled information about the various editions of the Gospel of Mark, and has brought to our attention the widespread esoteric tradition among the earliest believers in Jesus. It is known that the Gospel of Mark has gone through several stages in its compositional history, including its use of more primitive collections of sayings, stories, parables, an apocalypse, and a passion narrative, as well as the subsequent addition of two separate, longer endings to the last chapter. Furthermore, Matthew and Luke have made full-scale revisions of the Gospel of Mark by independently incorporating it into their own gospels. The Secret Gospel of Mark is additional evidence of the instability of gospel texts and gospel manuscripts in the first two centuries C.E. Clement of Alexandria states that the Carpocratians used an edition of the Secret Gospel of Mark which differed in a number of respects from the edition which Clement's own church used. Some of this divergent material he termed "falsifications." Clement also states that the Secret Gospel of Mark is an expansion of the (now canonical) Gospel of Mark. In fact, the precise opposite may well be the case: the canonical (or "public") Gospel of Mark appears to be an abridgment of the Secret Gospel of Mark. The first edition of Mark, which was written ca. 70 C.E., is no longer extant. The Secret Gospel of Mark was probably composed around the beginning of the second *century, most likely in Syria. Sometime thereafter our present edition of Mark, with only vestiges of the secret tradition still visible (Mark 4:11; 9:25–27; 10:21, 32, 38–39; 12:32–34; 14:51–52), took shape.*

In the gospel citations that follow, care should be taken to distinguish between the actual quotations of the text of the Secret Gospel of Mark *and Clement's own interpretive comments. The text is divided according to the page and line numbers of the Greek manuscript. The translation was made by Morton Smith* (Clement of Alexandria and a Secret Gospel of Mark).

The Secret Gospel of Mark

Folio 1, recto From the letters of the most holy Clement, the author of the Stromateis. To Theodore.

You did well in silencing the unspeakable teachings of the Carpocratians. For these are the "wandering stars" referred to in the prophecy, who wander from the narrow road of the commandments into a boundless abyss of the carnal and bodily sins. [5] For, priding themselves in knowledge, as they say, "of the deep things of Satan," they do not know that they are casting themselves away into "the nether world of the darkness" of falsity, and, boasting that they are free, they have become slaves of servile desires. Such men are to be opposed in all ways and altogether. For, even if they should say something true, one who loves the truth should not, even so, agree with them. For not all true things are the truth, nor should [10] that truth which merely seems true according to human opinions be preferred to the true truth, that according to the faith.

Now of the things they keep saying about the divinely inspired Gospel according to Mark, some are altogether falsifications, and others, even if they do contain some true elements, nevertheless are not reported truly. For the true things being mixed with inventions, are falsified, so that, as the saying goes, even the salt [15] loses it savor.

As for Mark, then, during Peter's stay in Rome he wrote an account of the Lord's doings, not, however, declaring all of them, nor yet hinting at the secret ones, but selecting what he thought most useful for increasing the faith of those who were being instructed. But when

Peter died a martyr, Mark came over to Alexandria, bringing both his own notes and those of Peter, [20] from which he transferred to his former book the things suitable to whatever makes for progress toward knowledge. Thus he composed a more spiritual Gospel for the use of those who were being perfected. Nevertheless, he yet did not divulge the things not to be uttered, nor did he write down the hierophantic teaching of the Lord, but to the stories already written he added yet others and, moreover, brought in certain [25] sayings of which he knew the interpretation would, as a mystagogue, lead the hearers into the innermost sanctuary of that truth hidden by seven veils. Thus, in sum, he prepared matters, neither grudgingly nor incautiously, in my opinion, and, dying, he left his composition to the church in 1, verso Alexandria, where it even yet is most carefully guarded, being read only to those who are being initiated into the great mysteries.

But since the foul demons are always devising destruction for the race of men, Carpocrates, instructed by them and using deceitful arts, [5] so enslaved a certain presbyter of the church in Alexandria that he got from him a copy of the secret Gospel, which he both interpreted according to his blasphemous and carnal doctrine and, moreover, polluted, mixing with the spotless and holy words utterly shameless lies. From this mixture is drawn off [10] the teaching of the Carpocratians.

To them, therefore, as I said above, one must never give way; nor, when they put forward their falsifications, should one concede that the secret Gospel is by Mark, but should even deny it on oath. For, "Not all true things are to be said to all men." For this reason the Wisdom of God, through Solomon, advises, "Answer the fool from his folly," [15] teaching that the light of the truth should be hidden from those who are mentally blind. Again it says, "From him who has not shall be taken away," and, "Let the fool walk in darkness." But we are "children of light," having been illuminated by "the dayspring" of the spirit of the Lord "from on high," and "Where the Spirit of the Lord is," it says, "there is liberty," for "All things are pure to the pure."

To you, therefore, I shall not hesitate to answer the questions you have asked, [20] refuting the falsifications by the very words of the Gospel. For example, after "And they were in the road going up to Jerusalem," and what follows, until "After three days he shall arise," the secret Gospel brings the following material word for word: "And they come into Bethany. And a certain woman whose brother had died was there. And, coming, she prostrated herself before Jesus and says to him, 'Son of David, [25] have mercy on me.' But the disciples rebuked her. And Jesus, being angered, went off with her into the garden where the tomb was, and **2, recto** straightway a great cry was heard from the tomb. And going near Jesus rolled away the stone from the door of the tomb. And straightway, going in where the youth was, he stretched forth his hand and raised him, seizing his hand. But the youth, looking upon him, loved him and [5] began to beseech him that he might be with him. And going out of the tomb they came into the house of the youth, for he was rich. And after six days Jesus told him what to do and in the evening the youth comes to him, wearing a linen cloth over his naked body. And he remained with him that night, for [10] Jesus taught him the mystery of the kingdom of God. And thence, arising, he returned to the other side of the Jordan."

After these words follows the text, "And James and John come to him," and all that section. But "naked man with naked man," and the other things about which you wrote, are not found.

And after the words, "And he comes into Jericho," the secret Gospel adds only, "And [15] the sister of the youth whom Jesus loved and his mother and Salome were there, and Jesus did not receive them." But the many other things about which you wrote both seem to be and are falsifications.

Now the true explanation and that which accords with the true philosophy . . .

Papyrus Egerton 2

Papyrus Egerton 2 (Pap. Egerton 2) *comprises three fragmentary papyrus leaves of a Greek codex composed of sayings, controversy stories, and miracle stories of Jesus. In its present condition,* Papyrus Egerton 2 *is untitled and has no ascription of authorship. It has been customarily referred to as the "Unknown Gospel." On paleographical grounds the papyrus has been assigned a date in the first half of the second century* C.E. *This makes it one of the two earliest preserved papyrus witnesses to the gospel tradition. It is, in fact, the earliest datable non-canonical gospel extant today. The three papyrus leaves are written on both front and back sides and are part of the evidence that enables scholars to conclude that bookmaking was developed by the earliest Christians. Only the preserved portions of the first two papyrus leaves are reproduced below; the third leaf is too fragmentary for translation. Discovered in Egypt, and first published in 1935,* Papyrus Egerton 2 *is conserved today in the British Museum in London.*

Papyrus Egerton 2 *may be divided into five sections. Because of the state of preservation of the papyrus, it is impossible to arrange the fragments in any sequential order. One is obliged, rather, to consider each saying and story as an independent piece of the gospel tradition.* Papyrus Egerton 2 *shares traditions associated with all four of the canonical gospels, but is especially closely related to the Gospel of John.*

The first section (the reverse side of fragment 1) contains a carefully composed controversy story involving Jesus and the rulers of the Jews over the interpretation of the Jewish scriptures and the authority of Moses. A comparison of this story with its close parallels in the Gospel of John (John 5:39, 45; 9:29) demonstrates that the story in Papyrus Egerton 2 *is more primitive than the expanded version in John. This fact suggests that* Papyrus Egerton 2 *either is the source of the story in*

John or independently draws from the same source as does the Gospel of John, preserving the source in its more original form.

The second section (comprising the opening nine lines of the front side of fragment 1) preserves the end of a story of an attempted arrest and stoning of Jesus. This may be the conclusion of the controversy story in section one, although the fragmentary state of the papyrus does not permit certainty. Here, too, there are close parallels with the Gospel of John (John 7:30; 10:31, 39), which has used this same tradition in two different contexts. The reference to "the hour" of Jesus' betrayal presupposes a passion narrative, and suggests that Papyrus Egerton 2 also included an account of the suffering and death of Jesus, which has been lost because of deterioration of the papyrus.

The third section (the remainder of the front side of fragment 1) contains a miracle story of Jesus' healing of a leper. A variant of this story is also preserved in two different places in the synoptic gospels (Mark 1:40–45 and parallels; Luke 17:11–19). The fourth section (the front side of fragment 2) contains a controversy story that deals with the question of the payment of tribute to one's rulers. Individual elements of this story have parallels in various parts of all four canonical gospels (John 3:2; Mark 12:13–17 and parallels; Luke 6:46), but the story itself is preserved independently of the canonical gospel texts. The fifth section (the reverse side of fragment 2) comprises a very fragmentary narrative account of a miracle of Jesus at the Jordan River.

Papyrus Egerton 2 is an important source of as well as witness to the development of gospel traditions. Its relationship to the sources of the Gospel of John bears close scrutiny, since it is clear that John has consistently expanded more primitive stories such as these, developing them into longer discourses and dialogues. Moreover, the attribution of a controversy between Jesus and certain Jewish opponents, which plays such an important role in the origins and development of the Johannine community, is also well documented in Papyrus Egerton 2. Thus, this papyrus provides additional evidence of the separation of the Johannine community from Judaism, and is another link in the tradition leading from the Judaism of Jesus' day into Johannine sectarianism. Since Papyrus Egerton 2 displays no dependence upon the gospels of the New Testament, its date of composition is not contingent upon that of these or any other documents which we now possess. Its earliest possible date of composition would be sometime in the middle of the first century, when the sayings and stories which underlie the New Testament first began to be produced in written form. The latest possible date would be early in the second century, shortly before the copy of the extant papyrus *fragment was made. Because this papyrus presents traditions in a less developed form than John does, it was probably composed in the second half of the first century, in Syria, shortly before the Gospel of John was written.*

The text is divided according to the page and line numbers (lines 1– 75) of the Greek manuscript. The translation was made by Joachim Jeremias and George Ogg (New Testament Apocrypha).

Papyrus Egerton 2

Fragment 1, **verso** (lines 1–20) . . . to the lawyer[s: ". . . e]very one who act[s contrary to the l]aw, but not me! . . . [5] . . . what he does, as he does it." [And] having turn[ed] to [the] rulers of the people he [sp]oke the following saying: "(Ye) search the scriptures in which ye think that ye have life; these are they [10] which bear witness of me. Do not think that I came to accuse [you] to my Father! There is one [that ac]cuses [you], even Moses, on whom ye have set your hope." And when they sa[15][id]: "We know that God [hath] spok[en] to Moses, but as for thee, we know not [whence thou art]," Jesus answered and said unto them: "Now (already) accusation is raised against [your] unbelief. [20] [No one o]therwise . . ."

Fragment 1, **recto** (lines 22–41) . . . [to gather] stones together to stone him. And the [rul]ers laid [25] their hands on him that they might arrest him and [deliver] him to the multitude. But they w[ere not able] to arrest him because the hour of his betrayal [was] not yet c[ome]. [30] But he himself, the Lord, escaped out of [their han]ds and turned away from them.

And behold a leper drew near [to him] and said: "Master Jesus, wandering with lepers and eating with [them was I(?)] [35] in the inn; I also [became] a le[per]. If [thou] therefore [wilt], I am made clean." Immediately the Lord [said to him]: "I will, be thou made clean." [And thereupon] the leprosy departed from him. [And the Lord [40] said to him]: "Go [thy way and show th]yself to the [priests] . . ."

Fragment 2, **recto** (lines 43–59) . . . [ca]me to him to put him to the pro[of] and to tempt him, whilst [they said]: [45] "Master Jesus, we know that thou art come [from God], for what thou doest bears a test[imony] (to thee which goes) beyond (that) of all the prophets. [Wherefore tell] us: is it admissible [to p]ay to the kings the (charges) appertaining to their rule? [Should we] pay [th]⁵⁰em or not?" But Jesus saw through their [in]tention, became [angry] and said to them: "Why call ye me with yo[ur mou]th Master and yet [do] not what I say? Well has Is[aiah] prophesied [concerning y]⁵⁵ou saying: This [people honours] me with the[ir li]ps but their heart is far from me; [their worship is] vain. [They teach] precepts [of men]."

Fragment 2 verso (lines 60–75) . . . ⁶⁰ . . . place shut in . . . it was laid beneath and invisible . . . its wealth imponderable(?). And as they were in perplexity at his strange question, ⁶⁵ Jesus on his way came [to the] bank of the [riv]er Jordan, stretched out [hi]s right hand, [fill]ed it with . . . and sowed . . . on the ⁷⁰ . . . And then . . . water . . . And . . . before [their eyes], brought fruit . . . much . . . to the jo⁷⁵[y(?)] . . .

The Gospel of Peter

The Gospel of Peter (Gos. Pet.) *is preserved in a fragment of a gospel text that contains a passion narrative, an epiphany story, a story of the empty tomb, and the introduction to a resurrection story. Discovered in 1886–87 at Akhmîm, in Upper Egypt, and first published in 1892, this fragment is extant in Greek in a manuscript that dates from the eighth or ninth century* C.E. *Today this manuscript is conserved in the Cairo Museum.*

Unfortunately, the entirety of the Gospel of Peter *has not been preserved. The extant fragment begins abruptly in the middle of a scene in the passion narrative; it ends even more abruptly, in midsentence, in what seems to be the introduction to an account of a resurrection appearance of Jesus. The ornamentation at the beginning and end of the manuscript indicates that this particular fragment is a copy of an earlier document that contained more of the original gospel text. Scholars have generally accepted the identification of this fragment, which presents Peter as its author, with the* Gospel of Peter *that was used by the Christians at Rhossus (a coastal city in Syria), and was known, read, and, for the most part, approved by Serapion (Bishop of Antioch, ca. 200* C.E.*). Since no quotations of that gospel have come down to us from antiquity, it cannot be conclusively determined whether references to a* Gospel of Peter, *which are recorded by the church historian Eusebius (early in the fourth century), are, indeed, references to that gospel which has been discovered in fragmentary form at Akhmîm. However, two Greek papyrus fragments from the late second or early third century, which were recently uncovered at Oxyrhynchus, Egypt, and published in 1972, seem to confirm the plausibility of this identification. These fragments contain a portion of the text of a* *passion narrative and appear to come from the* Gospel of Peter, *but from a recension that is different from that of the Akhmîm fragment. If so, this is the earliest extant evidence of an edition of the text of the* Gospel of Peter, *antedating the previously known text by over five hundred years. This Oxyrhynchus papyrus is conserved in the Ashmolean Museum, Oxford.*

Identification of the sources of the Gospel of Peter *is a matter of considerable debate. However, the language used to portray the passion provides a clue to the use of sources, the character of the tradition, and the date of composition. Analysis reveals that the passion narrative of the* Gospel of Peter *has been composed on the basis of references to the Jewish scriptures. The* Gospel of Peter *thus stands squarely in the tradition of exegetical interpretation of the Bible. Its source of the passion narrative is oral tradition, understood in the light of scripture, interpreted within the wisdom movement. This accords with what we know of the confessions of the earliest believers in Jesus: in the beginning, belief in the suffering, death, burial, and resurrection of Jesus was simply the conviction that all this took place "according to the scriptures" (I Cor. 15:3–5). In utilizing scriptural references to compose the work, the* Gospel of Peter *shows no knowledge of the special material distinctive to each of the four gospels now in the New Testament. The developed apologetic technique typical of the* Gospel of Matthew *and of Justin (a church writer who lived in the middle of the second century), which seeks to demonstrate a correspondence between so-called prophetic "predictions" in the scriptures and their "fulfillment" in the fate of Jesus, is lacking. The use of quotation formulas to introduce scriptural citations is also absent.*

All of this suggests that the Gospel of Peter *is an independent witness of gospel traditions. Its earliest possible date of composition would be in the middle of the first century, when passion narratives first began to be compiled. The latest possible date would be in the second half of the second century, shortly before this gospel was used by the Christians at Rhossus and the copy discovered at Oxyrhynchus was made. It is well known that the passion narrative which Mark used originally circulated independently of his gospel; the* Gospel of John *demonstrates that different versions of this early passion narrative were in circulation. It is possible that the* Gospel of Peter *used a source similar to that preserved independently in Mark and John. The basic stories underlying the accounts of the epiphany and the empty tomb are form-critically discrete and probably very old. In fact, these stories are closely related to certain legendary accounts and apologetic fragments that intrude into the gospels of the New Testament (Matt. 27:51–54, 62–66; 28:2–4; Mark 9:2–8 and parallels). The Gospel of Peter's exoneration of Pilate, the Roman procurator who had Jesus killed, and the accompanying anti-Jewish polemic are secondary additions to these primitive narratives, imported from a situation in which the Jesus movement was beginning to define itself in opposition to other Jewish communities.*

Form criticism and redaction criticism indicate that the Gospel of Peter was dependent upon a number of sources, but it is quite possible that the document as we have it antedates the four gospels of the New Testament and may have served as a source for their respective authors. The Gospel of Peter was probably composed in the second half of the first century, most likely in western Syria. As such, it is the oldest extant writing produced and circulated under the authority of the apostle Peter. The creation of a passion and resurrection narrative was the product of a community of believers who understood the ultimate activity of God to have taken place in their own time, when the powers of unrighteousness and death were conquered by God's definitive act of raising the dead. Accordingly, the fate of Jesus is interpreted, in the hindsight of scripture, as God's vindication of the suffering righteous one.

The text is numbered according to chapter and verse divisions (1.1–14.60). The translation was made by Christian Maurer and George Ogg (New Testament Apocrypha).

The Gospel of Peter

---

1. 1. But of the Jews none washed their hands, neither Herod nor any one of his judges. And as they would not wash, Pilate arose. 2. And then Herod the king commanded that the Lord should be marched off, saying to them, "What I have commanded you to do to him, do ye."

2. 3. Now there stood there Joseph, the friend of Pilate and of the Lord, and knowing that they were about to crucify him he came to Pilate and begged the body of the Lord for burial. 4. And Pilate sent to Herod and begged his body. 5. And Herod said, "Brother Pilate, even if no one had begged him, we should bury him, since the Sabbath is drawing on. For it stands written in the law: the sun should not set on one that has been put to death."

And he delivered him to the people on the day before the unleavened bread, their feast. 3. 6. So they took the Lord and pushed him in great haste and said, "Let us hale the Son of God now that we have gotten power over him." 7. And they put upon him a purple robe and set him on the judgment seat and said, "Judge righteously, O King of Israel!" 8. And one of them brought a crown of thorns and put it on the Lord's head. 9. And others who stood by spat on his face, and others buffeted him on the cheeks, others nudged him with a reed, and some scourged him, saying, "With such honour let us honour the Son of God."

4. 10. And they brought two malefactors and crucified the Lord in the midst between them. But he held his peace, as if he felt no pain. 11. And when they had set up the cross, they wrote upon it: this is the King of Israel. 12. And they laid down his garments before him and divided them among themselves and cast the lot upon them. 13. But one of the malefactors rebuked them, saying, "We have landed in suffering for the deeds of wickedness which we have committed, but this man, who has become the saviour of men, what wrong has he done you?" 14. And they were wroth with him and commanded that his legs should not be broken, so that he might die in torments.

5. 15. Now it was midday and a darkness covered all Judaea. And they became anxious and uneasy lest the sun had already set, since he was still alive. <For> it stands written for them: the sun should not set on one that has been put to death. 16. And one of them said, "Give him to drink gall with vinegar." And they mixed it and gave him to drink. 17. And they fulfilled all things and completed the measure of their sins on their head. 18. And many went about with lamps, <and> as they supposed that it was night, they went to bed (or: they stumbled). 19. And the Lord called out and cried, "My power, O power, thou hast forsaken me!" And having said this he was taken up. 20. And at the same hour the veil of the temple in Jerusalem,was rent in two.

6. 21. And then the Jews drew the nails from the hands of the Lord and laid him on the earth. And the whole earth shook and there came a great fear. 22. Then the sun shone <again>, and it was found to be the ninth hour. 23. And the Jews rejoiced and gave his body to Joseph that he might bury it, since he had seen all the good that he (Jesus) had

done. 24. And he took the Lord, washed him, wrapped him in linen and brought him into his own sepulchre, called Joseph's Garden.

7. 25. Then the Jews and the elders and the priests, perceiving what great evil they had done to themselves, began to lament and to say, "Woe on our sins, the judgment and the end of Jerusalem is drawn nigh." 26. But I mourned with my fellows, and being wounded in heart we hid ourselves, for we were sought after by them as evildoers and as persons who wanted to set fire to the temple. 27. Because of all these things we were fasting and sat mourning and weeping night and day until the Sabbath.

8. 28. But the scribes and Pharisees and elders, being assembled together and hearing that all the people were murmuring and beating their breasts, saying, "If at his death these exceeding great signs have come to pass, behold how righteous he was!",—29. were afraid and came to Pilate, entreating him and saying, 30. "Give us soldiers that we may watch his sepulchre for three days, lest his disciples come and steal him away and the people suppose that he is risen from the dead, and do us harm." 31. And Pilate gave them Petronius the centurion with soldiers to watch the sepulchre. And with them there came elders and scribes to the sepulchre. 32. And all who were there, together with the centurion and the soldiers, rolled thither a great stone and laid it against the entrance to the sepulchre 33. and put on it seven seals, pitched a tent and kept watch. 9. 34. Early in the morning, when the Sabbath dawned, there came a crowd from Jerusalem and the country round about to see the sepulchre that had been sealed.

35. Now in the night in which the Lord's day dawned, when the soldiers, two by two in every watch, were keeping guard, there rang out a loud voice in heaven, 36. and they saw the heavens opened and two men come down from there in a great brightness and draw nigh to the sepulchre. 37. That stone which had been laid against the entrance to the sepulchre started of itself to roll and gave way to the side, and the sepulchre was opened, and both the young men entered in. 10. 38. When now those soldiers saw this, they awakened the centurion and the elders—for they also were there to assist at the watch. 39. And whilst they were relating what they had seen, they saw again three men come out from the sepulchre, and two of them sustaining the other, and a cross following them, 40. and the heads of the two reaching to heaven, but that of him who was led of them by the hand overpassing the heavens. 41. And they heard a voice out of the heavens crying, "Thou hast preached to them that sleep," 42. and from the cross there

was heard the answer, "Yea." 11. 43. Those men therefore took counsel with one another to go and report this to Pilate. 44. And whilst they were still deliberating, the heavens were again seen to open, and a man descended and entered into the sepulchre. 45. When those who were of the centurion's company saw this, they hastened by night to Pilate, abandoning the sepulchre which they were guarding, and reported everything that they had seen, being full of disquietude and saying, "In truth he was the Son of God." 46. Pilate answered and said, "I am clean from the blood of the Son of God, upon such a thing have you decided." 47. Then all came to him, beseeching him and urgently calling upon him to command the centurion and the soldiers to tell no one what they had seen. 48. "For it is better for us," they said, "to make ourselves guilty of the greatest sin before God than to fall into the hands of the people of the Jews and be stoned." 49. Pilate therefore commanded the centurion and the soldiers to say nothing.

12. 50. Early in the morning of the Lord's day Mary Magdalene, a woman disciple of the Lord—for fear of the Jews, since (they) were inflamed with wrath, she had not done at the sepulchre of the Lord what women are wont to do for those beloved of them who die—took 51. with her her women friends and came to the sepulchre where he was laid. 52. And they feared lest the Jews should see them, and said, "Although we could not weep and lament on that day when he was crucified, yet let us now do so at his sepulchre. 53. But who will roll away for us the stone also that is set on the entrance to the sepulchre, that we may go in and sit beside him and do what is due?—54. For the stone was great,—and we fear lest any one see us. And if we cannot do so, let us at least put down at the entrance what we bring for a memorial of him and let us weep and lament until we have again gone home." 13. 55. So they went and found the sepulchre opened. And they came near, stooped down and saw there a young man sitting in the midst of the sepulchre, comely and clothed with a brightly shining robe, who said to them, 56. "Wherefore are ye come? Whom seek ye? Not him that was crucified? He is risen and gone. But if ye believe not, stoop this way and see the place where he lay, for he is not here. For he is risen and is gone thither whence he was sent." 57. Then the women fled affrighted.

14. 58. Now it was the last day of unleavened bread and many went away and repaired to their homes, since the feast was at an end. 59. But we, the twelve disciples of the Lord, wept and mourned, and each one, very grieved for what had come to pass, went to his own home.

60. But I, Simon Peter, and my brother Andrew took our nets and went to the sea. And there was with us Levi, the son of Alphaeus, whom the Lord . . .

The Gospel of the Hebrews

The Gospel of the Hebrews (Gos. Heb.) *is a syncretistic, Jewish-Christian document, composed in Greek, which presents traditions of Jesus' preexistence and coming into the world, his baptism and temptation, some of his sayings, and the report of a resurrection appearance to his brother, James the Just. This is the Jewish-Christian gospel most frequently mentioned by name in the early church; it is also the only one whose original title has been transmitted from antiquity. The title seems to indicate the identity of the group who used this gospel, and may suggest that this was the gospel of predominately Greek-speaking Jewish Christians. The* Gospel of the Hebrews *has no connection with other Jewish-Christian gospels, displaying no kinship with the Gospel of Matthew. It is instructive to note that most of the extant fragments come from quotations in the writings of persons who lived in Alexandria, Egypt.*

The Gospel of the Hebrews *may have been known to Papias (a church writer who died ca. 130 C.E., whose five-volume "Exegesis of the Sayings of the Lord" is now lost, preserved only in a few quotations in the writings of Eusebius). Hegesippus (late in the second century) and Eusebius (early in the fourth century) attest to the existence of this gospel, but do not quote from it. Fragments are preserved in the writings of Clement of Alexandria (late in the second century), Origen (early in the third century), and Cyril (Bishop of Jerusalem, ca. 350 C.E.). Jerome (ca. 400 C.E.) also preserves several fragments, all of which he probably reproduced from the writings of Origen. The extent of this gospel is no longer known. According to the list of "canonical" and "apocryphal" books drawn up by Nicephorus (Patriarch of Constantinople, 806–818 C.E.), the* Gospel of the Hebrews *contained 2200 lines, only 300 fewer than Matthew!*

The report of a resurrection appearance of Jesus to his brother, James, indicates the position of authority assigned to James in the Gospel of the Hebrews. It is well known that James was the leading figure of the conservative Jewish church in Jerusalem. Reports of his "conversion" by a vision of the risen Lord are well documented in the church (compare I Cor. 15:7), and are based on an early, probably sound tradition. According to the report in the Gospel of the Hebrews, James was the very first witness of the resurrection, and thus its principal guarantor. He is so distinguished that he is even said to have taken part in the Last Supper of Jesus. The esteem in which James is held in this gospel may be used to locate the authority and secure the identity of the tradition of those communities which appealed to him as their leader.

The accounts of Jesus' preexistence, coming, baptism, and temptation are abbreviated mythological narratives. They presuppose a myth of the descent of divine Wisdom, embodying herself definitively in a representative of the human race for the revelation and redemption of humankind. Such a myth was widespread in the Greco-Roman world and underlies many of the earliest christological formulations of believers in Jesus, as evidenced, for example, in Pauline (Phil. 2:6–11), synoptic (Matt. 11:25–30; Luke 7:18–35; 11:49–51), and Johannine traditions (John 1:1–18), as well as in those of the Gospel of Thomas. Moreover, the second saying of the Gospel of Thomas is also cited as part of the Gospel of the Hebrews, suggesting that this was a free-floating saying at home in Egypt as well as in Syria. The wisdom saying numbered below as fragment 5 may permit the suggestion that the majority of the sayings in the Gospel of the Hebrews had the same character as those of the synoptic gospels.

The extant fragments of the Gospel of the Hebrews display no dependence upon the writings of the New Testament. Unfortunately, it cannot be determined whether other portions of the text that are no longer preserved are in any way contingent upon these or any other writings which we now possess. The earliest possible date of the composition of the Gospel of the Hebrews would be in the middle of the first century, when Jesus traditions were first being produced and collected as part of the wisdom tradition. The latest possible date would be in the middle of the second century, shortly before the first reference to this gospel by Hegesippus and the quotations of it by Clement and Origen. Based on the parallels in the morphology of the tradition, an earlier date of composition is more likely than a later one. Internal evidence and external attestations indicate that Egypt was its place of origin.

In the gospel citations that follow, care should be taken to distinguish between the actual quotations of the text of the Gospel of the Hebrews *and the interpretive comments of the church writers who recorded the citations.*

The text is listed by the number of the preserved fragments (1–7). The translation was made by Philipp Vielhauer and George Ogg (New Testament Apocrypha).

The Gospel of the Hebrews

1. It is written in the Gospel of the Hebrews:
    When Christ wished to come upon the earth to men, the good Father summoned a mighty power in heaven, which was called Michael, and entrusted Christ to the care thereof. And the power came into the world and it was called Mary, and Christ was in her womb seven months.
    (Cyril of Jerusalem, *Discourse on Mary Theotokos* 12a)

2. According to the Gospel written in the Hebrew speech, which the Nazaraeans read, the whole fount of the Holy Spirit shall descend upon him . . . Further in the Gospel which we have just mentioned we find the following written:
    And it came to pass when the Lord was come up out of the water, the whole fount of the Holy Spirit descended upon him and rested on him and said to him: My son, in all the prophets was I waiting for thee that thou shouldest come and I might rest in thee. For thou art my rest; thou art my first-begotten Son that reignest for ever.
    (Jerome, *Commentary on Isaiah* 4 [on Isaiah 11:2])

3. And if any accept the Gospel of the Hebrews—here the Savior says:
    Even so did my mother, the Holy Spirit, take me by one of my hairs and carry me away on to the great mountain Tabor.
    (Origen, *Commentary on John* 2.12.87 [on John 1:3])

4a. As also it stands written in the Gospel of the Hebrews:

He that marvels shall reign, and he that has reigned shall rest.
(Clement, *Stromateis* 2.9.45.5)

4b. To those words (from Plato, *Timaeus* 90) this is equivalent:
He that seeks will not rest until he finds; and he that has found
shall marvel; and he that has marvelled shall reign; and he that has
reigned shall rest.
(Ibid., 5.14.96.3)

5. As we have read in the Hebrew Gospel, the Lord says to his
disciples:
And never be ye joyful, save when ye behold your brother with
love.
(Jerome, *Commentary on Ephesians* 3 [on Ephesians 5:4])

6. In the Gospel according to the Hebrews, which the Nazaraeans
are wont to read, there is counted among the most grievous
offences:
He that has grieved the spirit of his brother.
(Jerome, *Commentary on Ezekiel* 6 [on Ezekiel 18:7])

7. The Gospel called according to the Hebrews which was recently
translated by me into Greek and Latin, which Origen frequently
uses, records after the resurrection of the Savior:
And when the Lord had given the linen cloth to the servant of
the priest, he went to James and appeared to him. For James had
sworn that he would not eat bread from that hour in which he had
drunk the cup of the Lord until he should see him risen from
among them that sleep. And shortly thereafter the Lord said: Bring
a table and bread! And immediately it is added: he took the bread,
blessed it and brake it and gave it to James the Just and said to him:
My brother, eat thy bread, for the Son of man is risen from among
them that sleep.
(Jerome, *De viris inlustribus* 2)

"John's Preaching of the Gospel," The Acts of John 87–105

The Acts of John (Acts John) *is a literary romance comprising several discrete pieces of tradition about the alleged activities of the apostle John. Many of its stories circulated orally before they found their way into various Greek manuscripts and a variety of ancient translations under the title the* Acts of John. *The section generally referred to today as "John's Preaching of the Gospel," which constitutes chapters 87–105 of the present edition of the text, presents a docetic interpretation of the earthly appearances of Jesus and of the meaning of the cross. This is given in the form of a homiletic narrative in the first person, and is attributed to the apostle John, identified here as one of the sons of Zebedee (compare Mark 1:16–20 and parallels). This section is extant in a single Greek manuscript from Vienna that was uncovered in 1886 and first published in 1897; a scribal note in the manuscript explains that it was copied in 1324 C.E. The section itself is much earlier: Augustine quoted a fragment of it in a letter that he wrote in the fifth century, and portions of it were read and condemned as heretical at the Second Nicene Council of 787. The lost original, from which the Vienna manuscript ultimately stems, is one of the literary sources used by the compiler of the entire* Acts of John.

The oldest portion of "John's Preaching of the Gospel" is a hymn now embedded in the text. The presence of certain liturgical instructions and of the responsory "Amen" in the hymn demonstrates that this hymn had a liturgical function in the life of the Johannine community. Many of the terms in the hymn have parallels in the Prologue of the Gospel of John (John 1:1–18). Whether this hymn is dependent upon the Gospel of John, or whether it is derived from the common source of traditions

*from which the author of John received a similar hymn which he utilized
in composing the Prologue, is still an open question. The gnosticizing
tendency of the Johannine tradition which produced and used this
hymn is made explicit here: the believer is to recognize himself in the
revealer; by understanding who Jesus is, the believer will come to know
himself.*

*This gnostic inclination is developed in a different way in the
homiletic portions of "John's Preaching of the Gospel." The fundamen-
tal theological occasion for writing this entire piece is to present the
reality of Jesus as spiritual. According to this view, although Jesus may
have appeared as tangible flesh and blood, in reality he was pure spirit,
whose physical appearance was mere semblance, an optical illusion.
"John's Preaching of the Gospel" seeks to demonstrate this interpretation in a conscious defense of a "docetic" christology, in opposition to
other Christians who were attacking such christologies. Thus, an
antithesis is set up between the "real" heavenly Lord and the earthly
"phantom" who was crucified.*

*It has long been recognized that the Gospel of John is closely related
to the development of gnosticism; the earliest interpreters of John, as a
matter of fact, were gnostics. It was to combat as "heretical" the gnostic
interpretation of John, and to retrieve John's Gospel as the possession of
the "orthodox," that the first and third Epistles of John were written.
"John's Preaching of the Gospel" simply gives a more gnostic exposition
of the tendencies that are latent within the Gospel of John itself. Thus,
the collection of miracle stories (commonly called an aretalogy), which
underlies the narrative of Jesus' earthly appearances in "John's Preaching of the Gospel," is no longer concerned merely with the presence of
the risen Lord as the one who transcends the limitations of human life.
Instead, this narrative is anxious to demonstrate the literal transcen-
dence of earthly existence in the life of Jesus himself. "John's Preaching
of the Gospel" is evidence of the gnostic heritage of Johannine
Christianity.*

*The earliest possible date of the composition of this section of the Acts
of John would be in the second half of the first century, contemporary
with the date of the composition of the Gospel of John. The latest
possible date would be in the third century, when "apocryphal" Acts
were widely known and critically discussed, and before the first reference
to the entire Acts of John in the writings of Eusebius of Caesarea (early
in the fourth century). Internal evidence suggests a date of composition
early in the second century, in Syria, shortly after the Gospel of John*

was written and contemporary with the competitive circulation of the first and third Epistles of John.

The text is numbered according to chapter divisions (87–105). The numbering of the fifty-one lines of the hymn is also not in any manuscript but is in accordance with scholarly practice. The translation was made by Knut Schäferdiek and G. C. Stead (New Testament Apocrypha).

"John's Preaching of the Gospel," The Acts of John 87–105

87. Now those that were present enquired the cause, and were especially perplexed, because Drusiana has said, "The Lord appeared to me in the tomb in the form of John and in that of a young man." So since they were perplexed and in some ways not yet established in the faith, John took it patiently and said,

88. "Men and brethren, you have experienced nothing strange or incredible in your perception of the ⟨Lord⟩, since even we whom he chose to be his apostles have suffered many temptations; and I cannot ⟨either⟩ speak or write to you the things which I have seen and heard. Yet now I must adapt myself to your hearing and according to each man's capacity I will impart to you those things of which you can be hearers, that you may know the glory which surrounds him that was and is both now and evermore.

For when he had chosen Peter and Andrew, who were brothers, he came to me and to my brother James, saying 'I need you; come with me!' And my brother said this to me, 'John, what does he want, this child on the shore who called us?' And I said, 'Which child?' And he answered me, 'The one who is beckoning to us.' And I said, 'This is because of the long watch we have kept at sea. You are not seeing straight, brother James. Do you not see the man standing there who is handsome, fair, and cheerful-looking?' But he said to me, 'I do not see that man, my brother. But let us go, and we will see what this means.'

89. And when we had brought the boat to land we saw how he also

helped us to beach the boat. And as we left the place, wishing to follow
him, he appeared to me again as rather bald-⟨headed⟩ but with a thick
flowing beard, but to James as a young man whose beard was just
beginning. So we wondered both of us about the meaning of the vision
we had seen. Then as we both followed him we became gradually
⟨more⟩ perplexed about this matter.

huh

But then there appeared to me a yet more amazing sight; I tried to
see him as he was, and I never saw his eyes closing, but always open.
But he sometimes appeared to me as a small man with no good looks,
and then again as looking up to heaven. And he had another strange
(property); when I reclined at table he would take me to his own breast,
and I held him (fast); and sometimes his breast felt to me smooth and
soft, but sometimes hard like rock; so that I was perplexed in my (mind)
and said, 'Why do I find it so?' And as I thought about it, he . . .

90. Another time he took me and James and Peter to the mountain
where he used to pray, and we saw ⟨on⟩ him a light such that a man,
who uses mortal speech, cannot describe what it was like. Again he
took us three likewise up the mountain, saying 'Come with me.' And
again we went; and we saw him at a distance praying. Then I, since he
loved me, went quietly up to him, as if he could not see, and stood
looking at his hinder parts; and I saw him not dressed in clothes at all,
but stripped of those ⟨that⟩ we (usually) saw (upon him), and not like a
man at all. (And I saw that) his feet were whiter than snow, so that the
ground there was lit up by his feet; and that his head stretched up to
heaven, so that I was afraid and cried out; and he, turning about,
appeared as a small man and caught hold of my beard and pulled it
and said to me, 'John, do not be faithless, but believing, and not
inquisitive.' And I said to him, 'Why, Lord, what have I done? ' But I
tell you, my brethren, that I suffered such pain for thirty days in the
place where he touched my beard, that I said to him, 'Lord, if your
playful tug has caused such pain, what (would it be) if you had dealt
me a blow?' And he said to me, 'Let it be your concern from now on
not to tempt him that cannot be tempted.'

91. But Peter and James were vexed as I spoke with the Lord, and
beckoned me to come to them and leave the Lord alone. And I went,
and they both said to me, 'Who was it who spoke with the Lord when
he was on the (mountain-)top? For we heard them both speaking.' And
when I considered his abundant grace and his unity within many faces
and his unceasing wisdom that looks after us, I said, 'You shall learn
this from him if you ask him.'

92. And again when we—that is, all his disciples—were sleeping in one house at Gennesaret, I wrapped myself in my cloak and watched by myself (to see) what he was doing. And first I heard him say, 'John, go to sleep.' Then I pretended to sleep; and I saw another like him coming down, and I heard him also saying to my Lord, 'Jesus, the men you have chosen still disbelieve you.' And my Lord said to him, 'You are right; for they are men.'

93. I will tell you another glory, brethren; sometimes when I meant to touch him I encountered a material, solid body; but at other times again when I felt him, his substance was immaterial and incorporeal, and as if it did not exist at all.

And if ever he were invited by one of the Pharisees and went (where) he was invited, we went with him; and one loaf was laid before each one of us by those who had invited (us), and so he also would take one; but he would bless his and divide it among us; and every man was satisfied by that little (piece), and our loaves were kept intact, so that those who had invited him were amazed.

And I often wished, as I walked with him, to see his footprint in the earth, whether it appeared—for I saw him raising himself from the earth—and I never saw it. And I tell you this much, my brethren, so as to encourage your faith in him: for his miracles and wonderful works must not be told for the moment, for they are unspeakable and, perhaps, can neither be uttered nor heard.

94. But before he was arrested by the lawless Jews, whose lawgiver is the lawless serpent, he assembled us all and said, 'Before I am delivered to them, let us sing a hymn to the Father, and so go to meet what lies before (us).' So he told us to form a circle, holding one another's hands, and himself stood in the middle and said, 'Answer Amen to me.' So he began to sing the hymn and to say,

  1. 'Glory be to thee, Father.'
And we circled round him and answered him, 'Amen.'
   'Glory be to thee, Logos:
    Glory be to thee, Grace.'—'Amen.'
  2. 'Glory be to thee, Spirit:
   Glory be to thee, Holy One:
    Glory be to thy Glory.'—'Amen.'
  3. 'We praise thee, Father:
   We thank thee, Light:
    In whom darkness dwelleth not.'—'Amen.'

95. 'And why we give thanks, I tell you:
  4. 'I will be saved,
   And I will save.'—'Amen.'

   5. 'I will be loosed,
        And I will loose.'—'Amen.'
   6. 'I will be wounded,
        And I will wound.'—'Amen.'
   7. 'I will be born,
        And I will bear.'—'Amen.'
   8. 'I will eat,
        And I will be eaten.'—'Amen.'
   9. 'I will hear,
        And I will be heard.'—'Amen.'
  10. 'I will be thought,
        Being wholly thought.'—'Amen.'
  11. 'I will be washed,
        And I will wash.'—'Amen.'

Grace dances.
  12. 'I will pipe,
        Dance, all of you.'—'Amen.'
  13. 'I will mourn,
        Beat you all your breasts.'—'Amen.'
  14. '(The) one Ogdoad
        sings praises with us.'—'Amen.'
  15. 'The twelfth number
        dances on high.'—'Amen.'
  16. 'To the Universe
        belongs the dancer.'—'Amen.'
  17. 'He who does not dance
        does not know what happens.'—'Amen.'
  18. 'I will flee,
        and I will remain.'—'Amen.'
  19. 'I will adorn,
        and I will be adorned.'—'Amen.'
  20. 'I will be united,
        and I will unite.'—'Amen.'
  21. 'I have no house,
        and I have houses.'—'Amen.'
  22. 'I have no place,
        and I have places.'—'Amen.'
  23. 'I have no temple,
        and I have temples.'—'Amen.'

24. 'I am a lamp to you (sing.)
    who see me.'—'Amen.'
25. 'I am a mirror to you
    who know me.'—'Amen.'
26. 'I am a door to you
    ⟨who⟩ knock on me.'—'Amen.'
27. 'I am a way to you
    ⟨the⟩ traveller.'—⟨'Amen'⟩.

96. 28. 'Now if you follow
    my dance,
29. see yourself
    in Me who am speaking,
30. and when you have seen what I do,
    keep silence about my mysteries.
31. You who dance, consider
    what I do, for yours is
32. This passion of Man
    which I am to suffer.
33. For you could by no means
    have understood what you suffer
34. unless to you as Logos
    I had been sent by the Father.
35. You who saw what I suffer
    saw ⟨me⟩ as suffering ⟨yourself⟩,
36. and seeing it you did not stay
    but were wholly moved.
37. Being moved towards wisdom
    you have me as a support;
    rest in me.
38. Who I am, you shall know
    when I go forth.
39. What I now am seen to be,
    that I am not;
40. ⟨What I am⟩ you shall see
    when you come yourself.
41. If you knew how to suffer
    you would be able not to suffer.
42. Learn how to suffer
    and you shall be able not to suffer.
43. What you do not know
    I myself will teach you.

44. I am your God,
   not (the God) of the traitor.
45. I will that there be prepared
   holy souls for me.
46. Understand the word
   of wisdom!
47. As for me,
   if you would understand what I was:
48. By the word (?Word) I mocked at all things
   and I was not mocked at all,
49. I exulted:
   but do you understand the whole,
50. and when you have understood it, say,
   Glory be to thee, Father.

Say again with me,
51. Glory be to thee, Father,
   Glory be to thee, Word.
   Glory be to thee, {holy} Spirit.'—'Amen.'

97. After the Lord had so danced with us, my beloved, he went out. And we were like men amazed or fast asleep, and we fled this way and that. And so I saw him suffer, and did not wait by his suffering, but fled to the Mount of Olives and wept at what had come to pass. And when he was hung (upon the Cross) on Friday, at the sixth hour of the day there came a darkness over the whole earth. And my Lord stood in the middle of the cave and gave light to it and said, 'John, for the people below in Jerusalem I am being crucified and pierced with lances and reeds, and given vinegar and gall to drink. But to you I am speaking, and listen to what I speak. I put into your mind to come up to this mountain so that you may hear what a disciple should learn from his teacher and a man from God.'

98. And when he had said this he showed me a Cross of Light firmly fixed, and around the Cross a great crowd, which had no single form; and in it (the Cross) was one form and the same likeness. And I saw the Lord himself above the Cross, having no shape but only a kind of voice; yet not that voice which we knew, but one that was sweet and gentle and truly (the voice) of God, which said to me, 'John, there must (be) one man (to) hear these things from me; for I need one who is ready to hear. This Cross of Light is sometimes called Logos by me for your sakes, sometimes mind, sometimes Jesus, sometimes Christ, sometimes a door, sometimes a way, sometimes bread, sometimes seed, sometimes resurrection, sometimes Son, sometimes Father, sometimes Spirit, sometimes life, sometimes truth, sometimes faith, sometimes grace; and so (it is called) for men's sake.

But what it truly is, as known in itself and spoken to us, (is this): it is the distinction of all things, and the strong uplifting of what is firmly fixed out of what is unstable, and the harmony of wisdom, being wisdom in harmony (?). ⟨But⟩ there are ⟨places⟩ on the right and on the left, powers, authorities, principalities and the demons, activities, threatenings, passions, devils, Satan and the inferior root from which the nature of transient things proceeded.

99. This Cross then (is that) which has united all things by the word and which has separated off what is transitory and inferior, which has also compacted all things into ⟨one⟩. But this is not that wooden Cross which you shall see when you go down from here; nor am I the (man) who is on the Cross, (I) whom now you do not see but only hear (my) voice. I was taken to be what I am not, I who am not what for many others I was; but what they will say of me is mean and unworthy of me. Since then the place of (my?) rest is neither (to be) seen nor told, much more shall I, the Lord of this (place), be neither seen ⟨nor told⟩.

100. The multitude around the Cross that is ⟨not⟩ of one form is the inferior nature. And those whom you saw in the Cross, even if they have not (yet) one form—not every member of him who has come down has yet been gathered together. But when human nature is taken up, and the race that comes to me and obeys my voice, then he who now hears me shall be united with this (race) and shall no longer be what he now is, but (shall be) above them as I am now. For so long as you do not call yourself mine, I am not what I am; but if you hear me, you also as hearer shall be as I am, and I shall be what I was, when you (are) as I am with myself; for from me you are ⟨what I am⟩(?). Therefore ignore the many and despise those who are outside the mystery; for you must know that I am wholly with the Father, and the Father with me.

101. So then I suffered none of those things which they will say of me; even that suffering which I showed to you and to the rest in my dance, I will that it be called a mystery. For what you are, that I have shown you, (as) you see; but what I am is known to me alone, and no one else. Let me have what is mine; what is yours you must see through me; but me you must see truly—not ⟨that which⟩ I am, (as) I said, but that which you, as (my) kinsman, are able to know. You hear that I suffered, yet I suffered not; and that I suffered not, yet I did suffer; and that I was pierced, yet I was not wounded; that I was hanged, yet I was not hanged; that blood flowed from me, yet it did not flow; and, in a word, that what they say of me, I did not endure, but what they do not say, those things I did suffer. Now what these are, I secretly show you; for I know that you will understand. You must know me, then, as the torment of the Logos, the piercing of the Logos, the blood of the Logos, the wounding of the Logos, the fastening of the Logos, the death of the Logos. And so I speak, discarding the man(hood). The first then (that) you must know (is) the Logos; then you shall know the Lord, and thirdly the man, and what he has suffered.'

102. When he had said these things to me, and others which I know not how to say as he wills, he was taken up, without any of the multitude seeing him. And going ⟨down⟩ I laughed at them all, since he had told me what they had said about him; and I held this one thing fast in my (mind), that the Lord had performed everything as a symbol and a dispensation for the conversion and salvation of man.

103. Now, my brothers, since we have seen the grace of the Lord and his affection towards us, let us worship him, since we have obtained mercy from him; not with (our) fingers, nor with (our) mouths nor with (our) tongue nor with any member of (our) body at all, but with the disposition of our soul; (let us worship) him who was made man ⟨apart from⟩ this body. And let us watch, since he is at hand even now in prisons for our sakes, and in tombs, in bonds and dungeons, in reproaches and insults, by sea and on dry land, in torments, sentences, conspiracies, plots and punishments; in a word, he is with all of us, and with the sufferers he suffers himself, (my) brethren. If he is called upon by any of us he does not hold out against hearing us, but being everywhere he hears us all, and now also myself and Drusiana, being the God of those who are imprisoned, bringing us help through his own compassion.

104. You therefore, beloved, (must) also be persuaded, that it is not a man that I exhort you to worship, but God unchangeable, God invincible, God who is higher than all authority and all power and elder and stronger than all angels and (all) that are called creatures and all aeons. So if you hold fast to him and are built up upon him, you shall possess your soul indestructible."

105. And when John had delivered these things to the brethren, he went out with Andronicus to walk. And Drusiana followed at a distance with (them) all to see the things performed by him and to hear his word at all times in the Lord.

The Gospel of the Nazoreans

The Gospel of the Nazoreans (Gos. Naz.) *is an expanded version of the Gospel of Matthew which is preserved in fragmentary form in the quotations of early church writers and in the marginal notations of a group of thirty-six manuscripts of the Gospel of Matthew which date from the Middle Ages. Collectively, these manuscripts seem to derive from a single, "Zion Gospel" edition which probably was composed before 500* C.E. *Examination of all these fragments reveals that the* Gospel of the Nazoreans *(also spelled "Nazaraeans") is a translation into Aramaic or Syriac of the original Greek of the Gospel of Matthew. There is no evidence that this gospel preserves traditions that derive from an independent Aramaic source. In certain exegetical writings of the Middle Ages there are additional citations that possibly come from the* Gospel of the Nazoreans *as well. Their attribution is uncertain, however, and so they are omitted here; these citations were probably copied from gospel catenae and commentaries, and not from copies of the original text.*

The first reference to the Gospel of the Nazoreans *was made ca. 180* C.E. *by Hegesippus (a church writer whose five-volume "Memoirs" are now lost, preserved only in a few quotations in the writings of Eusebius). Fragments are preserved in the works of Origen (early in the third century) and Eusebius (early in the fourth century); Epiphanius (late in the fourth century) attests to the existence of this gospel, but does not quote from it. Most of the fragments that are to be assigned to the* Gospel of the Nazoreans *come from the writings of Jerome (ca. 400* C.E.*), who incorrectly identifies this gospel with the* Gospel of the Hebrews, *but who, his testimony notwithstanding, certainly had firsthand knowledge only of the* Gospel of the Nazoreans.

The original title of this gospel is unknown. The designation customary today was assigned for the first time by the exegetes of the Middle Ages. It is probable, however, that this was the gospel used since the second century by the Nazoreans, a group of Jewish Christians in western Syria. Apparently this document was originally referred to as "the gospel which the Nazoreans used" or, when identified by the language in which it was written, as the "Hebrew" or "Jewish" gospel.

In scope and in content the Gospel of the Nazoreans *is closely related to the Gospel of Matthew. This is demonstrated most clearly in the marginal readings of the medieval manuscripts: these variant readings are secondary developments of the Matthean text. They include citations of Matthew's infancy and passion narratives; the extent of these and other citations suggests that the text of Matthew was given in order in its entirety. The lack of a citation from the resurrection narrative appears to be coincidental, due simply to the fragmentary state of the preserved text. In addition to the expansions, illustrations, and annotations of the Greek text of Matthew, new material is introduced which, in some instances, reflects early traditions of sayings of Jesus.*

The Gospel of the Nazoreans *was composed sometime after the Gospel of Matthew and before the first attestation of the text by Hegesippus. Its provenance is most likely western Syria, where Matthew was probably composed and the Nazoreans were still at home in the fourth century. The theology reflected in the extant fragments is not at all "heretical," but is closely aligned with and dependent upon the developing theology of the emerging "catholic" church. The variant readings witness to the instability of gospel texts and gospel manuscripts in the first few centuries* C.E. *Most of all, the* Gospel of the Nazoreans *demonstrates the continuing use and expansion of gospel traditions within a group of Jewish Christians.*

In the gospel citations that follow, care should be taken to distinguish between the actual quotations of the text of the Gospel of the Nazoreans *and the interpretive comments of the church writers who recorded the citations.*

The text is listed by the number of the preserved fragments (1–23). The translation was made by Philipp Vielhauer and George Ogg (New Testament Apocrypha).

The Gospel of the Nazoreans

1. To these (citations in which Matthew follows not the Septuagint but the Hebrew original text) belong the two: "Out of Egypt have I called my son" and "For he shall be called a Nazaraean."

   (Jerome, *De viris inlustribus* 3)

2. Behold, the mother of the Lord and his brethren said to him: John the Baptist baptizes unto the remission of sins, let us go and be baptized by him. But he said to them: Wherein have I sinned that I should go and be baptized by him? Unless what I have said is ignorance (a sin of ignorance).

   (Jerome, *Adversus Pelagianos* 3.2)

3. The Jewish Gospel has not "into the holy city" but "to Jerusalem."

   (Variant to Matthew 4:5 in the "Zion Gospel" Edition)

4. The phrase "without a cause" is lacking in some witnesses and in the Jewish Gospel.

   (Variant to Matthew 5:22, ibid.)

5. In the so-called Gospel according to the Hebrews instead of "essential to existence" I found "*maḥar*," which means "of tomorrow," so that the sense is:

   Our bread of tomorrow—that is, of the future—give us this day.

   (Jerome, *Commentary on Matthew* 1 [on Matthew 6:11])

6. The Jewish Gospel reads here as follows:

   If ye be in my bosom and do not the will of my Father in heaven, I will cast you out of my bosom.

   (Variant to Matthew 7:5—or better to Matthew 7:21–23—in the "Zion Gospel" Edition)

7. The Jewish Gospel: (wise) more than serpents.

   (Variant to Matthew 10:16, ibid.)

8. The Jewish Gospel has: (the kingdom of heaven) is plundered.

   (Variant to Matthew 11:12, ibid.)

9. The Jewish Gospel: I thank thee.

(Variant to Matthew 11:25, ibid.)

10. In the Gospel which the Nazarenes and the Ebionites use, which we have recently translated out of Hebrew into Greek, and which is called by most people the authentic (Gospel) of Matthew, the man who had the withered hand is described as a mason who pleaded for help in the following words:

I was a mason and earned (my) livelihood with (my) hands; I beseech thee, Jesus, to restore to me my health that I may not with ignominy have to beg for my bread.

(Jerome, *Commentary on Matthew* 2 [on Matthew 12:13])

11. The Jewish Gospel does not have: three d(ays and nights).

(Variant to Matthew 12:40 in the "Zion Gospel" Edition)

12. The Jewish Gospel: corban is what you should obtain from us.

(Variant to Matthew 15:5, ibid.)

13. What is marked with an asterisk (i.e., Matthew 16:2–3) is not found in other manuscripts, also it is not found in the Jewish Gospel.

(Variant to Matthew 16:2–3, ibid.)

14. The Jewish Gospel: son of John.

(Variant to Matthew 16:17, ibid.)

15a. He (Jesus) said: If thy brother has sinned with a word and has made thee reparation, receive him seven times in a day. Simon his disciple said to him: Seven times in a day? The Lord answered and said to him: Yea, I say unto thee, until seventy times seven times. For in the prophets also after they were anointed with the Holy Spirit, the word of sin (sinful discourse?) was found.

(Jerome, *Adversus Pelagianos* 3.2)

15b. The Jewish Gospel has after "seventy times seven times": For in the prophets also, after they were anointed with the Holy Spirit, the word of sin (sinful discourse?) was found.

(Variant to Matthew 18:22 in the "Zion Gospel" Edition)

16. The other of the two rich men said to him: Master, what good thing must I do that I may live? He said to him: Man, fulfil the law and the prophets. He answered him: That have I done. He said to him: Go and sell all that thou possessest and distribute it

among the poor, and then come and follow me. But the rich man then began to scratch his head and it (the saying) pleased him not. And the Lord said to him: How canst thou say, I have fulfilled the law and the prophets? For it stands written in the law: Love thy neighbour as thyself; and behold, many of thy brethren, sons of Abraham, are begrimed with dirt and die of hunger—and thy house is full of many good things and nothing at all comes forth from it to them! And he turned and said to Simon, his disciple, who was sitting by him: Simon, son of Jona, it is easier for a camel to go through the eye of a needle than for a rich man to enter into the kingdom of heaven.

(Origen, *Commentary on Matthew* 15.14 [on Matthew 19:16–30])

17. In the Gospel which the Nazarenes use, instead of "son of Barachias" we have found written "son of Joiada."

    (Jerome, *Commentary on Matthew* 4 [on Matthew 23:35])

18. But since the Gospel (written) in Hebrew characters which has come into our hands enters the threat not against the man who had hid (the talent), but against him who had lived dissolutely— for he (the master) had three servants: one who squandered his master's substance with harlots and flute-girls, one who multiplied the gain, and one who hid the talent; and accordingly one was accepted (with joy), another merely rebuked, and another cast into prison—I wonder whether in Matthew the threat which is uttered after the word against the man who did nothing may refer not to him, but by epanalepsis to the first who had feasted and drunk with the drunken.

    (Eusebius, *Theophania* 22 [on Matthew 25:14–15])

19. The Jewish Gospel: And he denied and swore and damned himself.

    (Variant to Matthew 26:74 in the "Zion Gospel" Edition)

20. Barabbas . . . is interpreted in the so-called Gospel according to the Hebrews as "son of their teacher."

    (Jerome, *Commentary on Matthew* 4 [on Matthew 27:16])

21. But in the Gospel which is written in Hebrew characters we read not that the veil of the temple was rent, but that the lintel of the temple of wondrous size collapsed.

    (Jerome, *Epistula ad Hedybiam* 120.8)

22. The Jewish Gospel: And he delivered to them armed men that

they might sit over against the cave and guard it day and night.
(Variant to Matthew 27:65 in the "Zion Gospel" Edition)

23. He (Christ) himself taught the reason for the separations of souls
that take place in houses, as we have found somewhere in the
Gospel that is spread abroad among the Jews in the Hebrew
tongue, in which it is said:

I choose for myself the most worthy: the most worthy are those
whom my Father in heaven has given me.
(Eusebius, *Theophania* 4.12 [on Matthew 10:34–36])

The Gospel of the Ebionites

The Gospel of the Ebionites (Gos. Eb.) *is a gospel harmony preserved in a few quotations in the writings of Epiphanius (a church writer who lived at the end of the fourth century* C.E.*). The original title of this gospel is unknown. The designation customary today is based on the fact that this was the gospel probably used by the Ebionites, a group of Greek-speaking Jewish Christians who were prominent throughout the second and third centuries. Epiphanius incorrectly entitles this the "Hebrew" gospel, and alleges that it is an abridged, truncated version of the* Gospel of Matthew. *Whereas the* Gospel of the Ebionites *is indeed closely related to Matthew, examination of the extant fragments reveals that much of the text is a harmony, composed in Greek, of the Gospels of Matthew and Luke (and, probably, the Gospel of Mark as well). Although Ireneus (late in the second century) attests to the existence of this gospel, we are dependent solely upon the quotations given by Epiphanius for our knowledge of the contents of the text.*

Like Mark and the Synoptic Sayings Source, Q, the Gospel of the Ebionites *begins with the preaching of John the Baptist and the baptism of Jesus. But though Mark and Q did not know of any birth or infancy stories, the* Gospel of the Ebionites *did, for they were present in its written sources, Matthew and Luke. Evidently the Ebionite community chose to omit these stories from their gospel because the Ebionites rejected the virgin birth.*

The theology of the Ebionites can be detected in the other gospel fragments as well. Their gospel makes both John the Baptist and Jesus vegetarians: John's diet is said to consist exclusively of wild honey; and Jesus is made to say that, at the passover meal with his disciples, he does not desire to eat meat. In another context, Jesus makes a legal pronouncement in which he states that he has come to abolish sacrifices.

Together with the saying about the passover, this intimates a polemic against the Jewish Temple. Since the Gospel of the Ebionites *was written after the destruction of the Temple in Jerusalem in 70* C.E., *such a polemic may have been intended to address the problem of the continuation of Judaism as a religion. In this respect, this gospel is to be compared especially with Matthew, which also appears to reinterpret Jewish and Jesus traditions to provide, in part, a possible option for Jewish identity after the destruction of the Temple. In opposition to the views of emerging Pharisaic Judaism, both Matthew and the* Gospel of the Ebionites *seem to suggest that faithful Jews are those who have come to believe in Jesus, the true interpreter of the Law. In the* Gospel of the Ebionites, *accordingly, the twelve apostles have been commissioned by Jesus himself to be witnesses for Israel, representatives of the twelve tribes.*

The Gospel of the Ebionites *was composed sometime after the Gospels of Matthew and Luke and before the first reference to it in the writings of Ireneus (toward the end of the second century). A date of composition in the middle of the second century, when several other gospel harmonies were also being written, is most likely. Its provenance is probably Syria-Palestine, where the Ebionites were at home.*

The quotations below are given in the order of their citation by Epiphanius, not necessarily in the order of their occurrence in the gospel itself. Care should be taken to distinguish between the actual quotations of the text of the Gospel of the Ebionites *and Epiphanius' own interpretive comments.*

The text is listed by the number of the preserved fragments (1–7). The translation was made by Philipp Vielhauer and George Ogg (New Testament Apocrypha).

The Gospel of the Ebionites

1. In the Gospel that is in general use amongst them, which is called according to Matthew, which however is not whole (and) complete but forged and mutilated—they call it the Hebrew Gospel—it is reported:

   There appeared a certain man named Jesus of about thirty years of age, who chose us. And when he came to Capernaum, he entered into the house of Simon whose surname was Peter, and opened his mouth and said: As I passed the Lake of Tiberias, I chose John and James the sons of Zebedee, and Simon and Andrew and Thaddaeus and Simon the Zealot and Judas the Iscariot, and thee, Matthew, I called as thou didst sit at the receipt of custom, and thou didst follow me. You therefore I will to be twelve apostles for a testimony unto Israel.

(Epiphanius, *Panarion* 30.13.2–3)

2. And:

It came to pass that John was baptizing; and there went out to him Pharisees and were baptized, and all Jerusalem. And John had a garment of camel's hair and a leathern girdle about his loins, and his food, as it saith, was wild honey, the taste of which was that of manna, as a cake dipped in oil.

Thus they were resolved to pervert the word of truth into a lie and to put a cake in the place of locusts.

(Ibid., 30.13.4–5)

3. And the beginning of their Gospel runs:

It came to pass in the days of Herod the king of Judaea, <when Caiaphas was high priest,> that there came <one>, John <by name,> and baptized with the baptism of repentance in the river Jordan. It was said of him that he was of the lineage of Aaron the priest, a son of Zacharias and Elisabeth; and all went out to him.

(Ibid., 30.13.6)

4. And after much has been recorded it proceeds:

When the people were baptized, Jesus also came and was baptized by John. And as he came up from the water, the heavens were opened and he saw the Holy Spirit in the form of a dove that descended and entered into him. And a voice (sounded) from heaven that said: Thou art my beloved Son, in thee I am well pleased. And again: I have this day begotten thee. And immediately a great light shone round about the place. When John saw this, it saith, he saith unto him: Who art thou, Lord? And again a voice from heaven (rang out) to him: This is my beloved Son in whom I am well pleased. And then, it saith, John fell down before him and said: I beseech thee, Lord, baptize thou me. But he prevented him and said: Suffer it; for thus it is fitting that everything should be fulfilled.

(Ibid., 30.13.7–8)

5. Moreover they deny that he was a man, evidently on the ground of the word which the Savior spoke when it was reported to him: "Behold, thy mother and thy brethren stand without," namely:

Who is my mother and who are my brethren? And he stretched forth his hand towards his disciples and said: These are my brethren and mother and sisters, who do the will of my Father.

(Ibid., 30.14.5)

6. They say that he (Christ) was not begotten of God the Father, but created as one of the archangels . . . that he rules over the angels and all the creatures of the Almighty, and that he came and declared, as their Gospel, which is called (according to Matthew? according to the Hebrews?), reports:

I am come to do away with sacrifices, and if ye cease not from sacrificing, the wrath of God will not cease from you.

(Ibid., 30.16.4–5)

7. But they abandon the proper sequence of the words and pervert the saying, as is plain to all from the readings attached, and have let the disciples say:

Where wilt thou that we prepare for thee the passover? and him to answer to that:

Do I desire with desire at this Passover to eat flesh with you?

(Ibid., 30.22.4)

The Protevangelium of James

The Protevangelium of James (Prot. Jas.) *is an infancy gospel that gives an account of the birth and dedication of Mary, the mother of Jesus, and of the birth of Jesus. This document is extant in Greek in over one hundred thirty manuscripts, almost all of which are later than the tenth century* C.E. *Numerous translations into ancient languages have survived as well. These manuscripts give various titles to the work; the designation customary today, the* Protevangelium of James, *implies that most of the events recorded in this "initial gospel" of James occur prior to those recorded in the gospels of the New Testament. Apparently that was the meaning intended when the title was assigned by the first two editors of the text, one of whom published a Latin translation in 1552* C.E., *and the other, an edition of the original Greek in 1564. A Greek papyrus of the* Protevangelium of James *from the third century has been recently discovered and was published in 1958. Although this papyrus is the earliest manuscript of the text extant today, many of its readings seem to be secondary. The precise relationship of this manuscript to others within the vast textual tradition of the* Protevangelium of James *is not yet clear. Today this papyrus is conserved in the Bodmer Library in Geneva.*

The Protevangelium of James *is a composite document. Its sources are oral and written traditions, the Jewish scriptures, and the Gospels of Matthew and Luke. From oral tradition come the legends of the parents of Mary, her childhood and betrothal to Joseph, his piety and previous marriage, and certain elements of the story of Jesus' birth, including the presence of a midwife and the mythological motif of birth in a cave. In using written texts as sources, the* Protevangelium of James *stands in an exegetical school tradition, which assumed that what was written in the past was, in fact, written with the intention to be applicable in the present and the future. Interpretive expansions of scriptural texts were given in order to make these texts understandable and useful to subsequent generations.* Thus, the entirety of the Protevangelium of James *is steeped in the language of the Septuagint, the Greek translation of the Jewish scriptures.* Not only are individual words, phrases, and even whole paragraphs reminiscent of the Septuagint; such discrete forms as the hymn and lament of Anna also display conscious, direct "remembrance" of the stories recorded in the scriptures. In this respect, *the* Protevangelium of James *is to be compared especially with the Gospel of Luke, whose infancy narrative is carefully composed on the basis of scriptural references.*

Like Matthew and Luke, *the* Protevangelium of James *also makes use of other written documents in re-creating the legends of the infancy of Jesus. But whereas these other sources of Matthew and Luke no longer survive, two of the sources of the* Protevangelium of James *have been preserved from antiquity: the Gospels of Matthew and Luke themselves. They too are texts used as part of this "midrashic" exegetical tradition. Frequently the respective passages in Matthew and Luke are harmonized into a single story in the* Protevangelium of James; *in some instances the two texts are conflated. It is by combining composite traditions with a harmony of the synoptic infancy stories that the* Protevangelium of James *has constructed the dramatic scenes of its gospel. Authorship is attributed to James, who is identified here as the stepbrother of Jesus.*

The earliest possible date for the composition of the Protevangelium of James *would be in the middle of the second century, sometime after the composition and subsequent circulation of the Gospels of Matthew and Luke; the latest possible date would be early in the third century, before the first reference to the* Protevangelium of James *was recorded by Origen (in the first half of the third century) and the copy of the Bodmer papyrus was made. The most probable date is the former; this is suggested in part by the creation of a harmony of Matthew and Luke, gospels which were not yet known as written texts with "scriptural" authority. The existence of other gospel harmonies at this time serves to corroborate this date. Of particular importance for comparative purposes is the harmony of select portions of Matthew and Luke, including their infancy narratives, which was used by Justin (a church writer who came from the East and founded a school in Rome before his martyrdom ca.* 165 C.E.) *Identifying the provenance of the* Protevangelium of James, *on the other hand, is extremely difficult. Syria is perhaps most plausible, because so many other gospel harmonies have their origin there; but a location in Asia Minor, Rome, or even Egypt is not at all impossible.*

The Protevangelium of James is important not only for its use of the infancy narratives of Matthew and Luke but also for its veneration of Mary, the mother of Jesus. The plethora of Greek editions and wealth of ancient translations suggest that the Protevangelium of James was widely used in Christian liturgies, particularly in churches of the East. The importance given to Mary in this document has certainly been extremely significant for Christian piety, art, and meditation. In using and expanding the infancy narratives, the Protevangelium of James has carried forward the aretalogical tradition of the gospels, including in the traditional enumeration of heroic feats the birth of the holy family. The bucolic scenes in the narrative of Jesus' birth recall other stories of the birth of "divine men" in antiquity, and are part of that tradition of Christian propaganda which sought to demonstrate the superiority of Jesus among heroes and gods.

The text that follows is essentially a translation of the Bodmer papyrus, our earliest extant manuscript. Variant readings from other manuscripts are sometimes included as well. These are indicated in the text by their insertion within square brackets, which sometimes are also set in a parallel column on the right-hand side of the page.

The text is numbered according to chapter and verse divisions (1.1–25.1). The translation was made by Oscar Cullmann and A. J. B. Higgins (New Testament Apocrypha).

The Protevangelium of James

1. 1. In the "Histories of the Twelve Tribes of Israel" Joachim was a very rich (man), and he brought all his gifts for the Lord twofold; for he said in himself, What I bring in excess, shall be for the whole people, and what I bring for forgiveness [of my sins] shall be for the Lord, for a propitiation for me.

2. Now the great day of the Lord drew near, and the children of Israel were bringing their gifts. Then they stood before him, and Reubel [Reuben] also, saying: "It is not fitting for you to offer your gifts

first, because you have begotten no offspring in Israel." 3. Then Joachim became very sad, and went to the record of the twelve tribes of the people [and said]: "I have searched whether I am the only one who has not begotten offspring in Israel, and I have found of all the righteous that they had raised up offspring in Israel. And I remembered the patriarch Abraham that in his last days God gave him a son, Isaac." 4. And Joachim was very sad, and did not show himself to his wife, but betook himself into the wilderness; there he pitched his tent and fasted forty days and forty nights; and he said to himself, "I shall not go down either for food or for drink until the Lord my God visits me; prayer shall be my food and drink."

2. 1. Meanwhile Anna his wife uttered a twofold lamentation and gave voice to a twofold bewailing:

"I will bewail my widowhood,
and bewail my childlessness."

2. Now the great day of the Lord drew near, and Euthine [Judith] her maidservant said to her: "How long do you humble your soul, since the great day of the Lord is near, and you ought not to mourn. But take this headband, which the mistress of the work gave me; it is not fitting for me to wear it, because I am [your] slave and it bears a royal mark."

3. But Anna said: "Away from me! I did not do this. It is the Lord who has greatly humbled me. Who knows whether a deceiver did not give it to you, and you have come to make me share in your sin!" Euthine [Judith] answered: "Why should I curse you because you have not listened to me? The Lord God has shut up your womb, to give you no fruit in Israel."

4. And Anna was very sad; but she put off her mourning garments, cleansed her head, put on her bridal garments, and about the ninth hour went into her garden to walk there. And she saw a laurel tree and sat down beneath it and implored the Lord, saying: "O God of our fathers, bless me and hear my prayer, as thou didst bless the womb of Sarah [our mother Sarah] and gavest her a son, Isaac."

3. 1. And Anna sighed towards heaven, and saw a nest of sparrows in the laurel tree and immediately she made lamentation within herself:

"Woe to me, who begot me,
What womb brought me forth?
For I was born as a curse before them all and before the children
    of Israel,

And I was reproached, and they mocked me and thrust me out of
the temple of the Lord.
2. Woe is me, to what am I likened?
I am not likened to the birds of the heaven;
for even the birds of the heaven are fruitful before thee, O Lord.
Woe is me, to what am I likened?
I am not likened to the unreasoning [dumb] animals;
for even the unreasoning [dumb] animals are fruitful before thee,
    O Lord.
Woe is to me, to what am I likened?
I am not likened to the beasts of the earth;
for even the beasts of the earth are fruitful before thee, O Lord.
3. Woe is me, to what am I likened?
I am not likened to these waters;
for even these waters gush forth merrily, and their fish praise thee,
    O Lord.
Woe is me, to what am I likened?
I am not likened to this earth;
for even this earth brings forth its fruit in its season and praises
    thee, O Lord."
4. 1. And behold an angel of the Lord came to her and said: "Anna,
Anna, the Lord has heard your prayer. You shall conceive and bear,
and your offspring shall be spoken of in the whole world." And Anna
said: "As the Lord my God lives, if I bear a child, whether male or
female, I will bring it as a gift to the Lord my God, and it shall serve
him all the days of its life."
2. And behold there came two messengers, who said to her:
"Behold, Joachim your husband is coming with his flocks; for an angel
of the Lord came down to him and said to him, 'Joachim, Joachim,
the Lord God has heard your prayer. Go down; behold, your wife
Anna has conceived [shall conceive].' " 3. And Joachim went down
and called his herdsmen and said: "Bring me ten lambs without
blemish and without spot; they shall belong to the Lord my God. And
bring me twelve [tender] calves for the priests and elders, and a
hundred kids for the whole people." 4. And behold Joachim came
with his flocks, and Anna stood at the gate and saw Joachim coming
and ran immediately and hung on his neck, saying: "Now I know that
the Lord God has greatly blessed me; for behold the widow is no longer
a widow, and I, who was childless, have conceived [shall conceive]."
And Joachim rested the first day in his house.

5. 1. But the next day he offered his gifts, saying in himself: "If the
Lord God is gracious to me the frontlet of the priest will make it clear
to me."

And Joachim offered his gifts, and observed the priest's frontlet when
he went up to the altar of the Lord; and he saw no sin in himself. And
Joachim said: "Now I know that the Lord God is gracious to me and
has forgiven all my sins." And he went down from the temple of the
Lord justified, and went to his house.

2. And her six months [her months] were fulfilled, as (the angel) had
said; in the seventh [ninth] month Anna brought forth. And she said to
the midwife: "What have I brought forth?" And she said: "A female."
And Anna said: "My soul is magnified this day." And she lay down.
And when the days were fulfilled, Anna purified herself from her
childbed and gave suck to the child, and called her Mary.

6. 1. Day by day the child waxed strong; when she was six months
old her mother stood her on the ground to try if she could stand. And
she walked [twice] seven steps and came to her bosom. And she took
her up, saying: "As the Lord my God lives, you shall walk no more
upon this ground until I take you into the temple of the Lord." And
she made a sanctuary in her bedchamber, and did not permit anything
common or unclean to pass through it. And she summoned the
undefiled daughters of the Hebrews, and they cared for her amuse-
ment.

2. On the child's first birthday Joachim made a great feast, and
invited the chief priests and the priests and the scribes and the elders
and the whole people of Israel. And Joachim brought the child to the
priests, and they blessed her, saying: "O God of our fathers, bless this
child and give her a name renowned for ever among all generations."
And all the people said: "So be it, [so be it,] Amen." And they brought
her to the chief priests, and they blessed her, saying: "O God of the
heavenly heights, look upon this child and bless her with a supreme
and unsurpassable blessing." And her mother carried her into the
sanctuary of her bedchamber and gave her suck. And Anna sang this
song to the Lord God:

"I will sing praises to the Lord my God,
for he has visited me and taken away from me the reproach of my
   enemies.
And the Lord gave me the fruit of righteousness, unique and
   manifold before him.
Who will proclaim to the sons of Reubel [Reuben] that Anna
   gives suck?

[Hearken, hearken, you twelve tribes of Israel: Anna gives suck.]"
And she laid the child down to rest in the bedchamber with its
sanctuary, and went out and served them. When the feast was ended
they went down rejoicing and glorifying the God of Israel.

7. 1. The months passed, and the child grew. When she was two
years old, Joachim said to Anna: "Let us bring her up to the temple of
the Lord, that we may fulfill the promise which we made, lest the Lord
send (some evil) upon us and our gift become unacceptable." And
Anna replied: "Let us wait until the third year, that the child may then
no more long after her father and mother." And Joachim said: "Very
well." 2. And when the child was three years old, Joachim said: "Let
us call the undefiled daughters of the Hebrews, and let each one take a
lamp, and let these be burning, in order that the child may not turn
back and her heart be enticed away from the temple of the Lord." And
he did so until they went up to the temple of the Lord. And the priest
took her and kissed her and blessed her, saying: "The Lord has
magnified your name among all generations; because of you the Lord
at the end of the days will manifest his redemption to the children of
Israel." 3. And he placed her on the third step of the altar, and the
Lord God put grace upon the child, and she danced for joy with her
feet, and the whole house of Israel loved her.

8. 1. And her parents went down wondering, praising and glorifying
the almighty God because the child did not turn back [to them]. And
Mary was in the temple nurtured like a dove and received food from
the hand of an angel. 2. When she was twelve years old, there took
place a council of the priests, saying, "Behold, Mary has become
twelve years old in the temple of the Lord. What then shall we do with
her, that she may not pollute the temple of the Lord?" And they said to
the high priest: "You stand at the altar of the Lord; enter (the
sanctuary) and pray concerning her, and what the Lord shall reveal to
you we will do." 3. And the high priest took the vestment with the
twelve bells and went into the Holy of Holies and prayed concerning
her. And behold, an angel of the Lord (suddenly) stood before him and
said to him: "Zacharias, Zacharias, go out and assemble the widowers
of the people, [who shall each bring a rod,] and to whomsoever the
Lord shall give a (miraculous) sign, his wife she shall be." And the
heralds went forth and spread out through all the country round about
Judaea; the trumpet of the Lord sounded, and all ran to it.

9. 1. And Joseph threw down his axe and went out to meet them.
And when they were gathered together, they took the rods and went to
the high priest. He took the rods of all and entered the temple and

prayed. When he had finished the prayer he took the rods, and went out (again) and gave them to them; but there was no sign on them. Joseph received the last rod, and behold, a dove came out of the rod and flew on to Joseph's head. And the priest said to Joseph: "Joseph, to you has fallen the good fortune to receive the virgin of the Lord; take her under your care." 2. (But) Joseph answered him: "I (already) have sons and am old, but she is a girl. I fear lest I should become a laughing-stock to the children of Israel." And the priest said to Joseph: "Fear the Lord thy God, and remember all that God did to Dathan, Abiram and Korah, how the earth was rent open and they were all swallowed up because of their rebellion. And now fear, Joseph, lest this happen (also) in your house." And Joseph was afraid, and took her under his care. And Joseph said to her: "Mary, I have received you from the temple of the Lord, and now I leave you in my house and go away to build my buildings; (afterwards) I will come (again) to you; the Lord will watch over you."

10. 1. Now there was a council of the priests, who resolved: "Let us make a veil for the temple of the Lord." And the priest said: "Call to me pure virgins of the tribe of David." And the officers departed and searched, and they found seven (such) virgins. And the priest remembered the child Mary, that she was of the tribe of David and was pure before God. And the officers went and fetched her. 2. Then they brought them into the temple of the Lord, and the priest said: "Cast me lots, who shall weave the gold, the amiant, the linen, the silk, the hyacinth-blue, the scarlet and the pure purple." And to Mary fell the lot of the "pure purple" and "scarlet." And she took them and worked them in her house. At that time Zacharias became dumb, and Samuel took his place until Zacharias was able to speak (again). But Mary took the scarlet and spun it.

11. 1. And she took the pitcher and went forth to draw water, and behold, a voice said: "Hail, thou that art highly favoured, [the Lord is with thee, blessed art thou] among women." And she looked around on the right and on the left to see whence this voice came. And trembling she went to her house and put down the pitcher and took the purple and sat down on her seat and drew out (the thread). 2. And behold, an angel of the Lord (suddenly) stood before her and said: "Do not fear, Mary; for you have found grace before the Lord of all things and shall conceive of his Word." When she heard this she doubted in herself and said: "Shall I conceive of the Lord, the living God, [and bear] as every woman bears?" 3. And the angel of the Lord said: "Not

so, Mary; for a power of the Lord shall overshadow you; wherefore also that holy thing which is born of you shall be called the Son of the Highest. And you shall call his name Jesus; for he shall save his people from their sins." And Mary said: "Behold, (I am) the handmaid of the Lord before him: be it to me according to your word."

12. 1. And she made (ready) the purple and the scarlet and brought (them) to the priest. And the priest took (them), and blessed (Mary) and said: "Mary, the Lord God has magnified your name, and you shall be blessed among all generations of the earth." 2. And Mary rejoiced, and went to Elizabeth her kinswoman, and knocked on the door. When Elizabeth heard it, she put down the scarlet, and ran to the door and opened it, [and when she saw Mary,] she blessed her and said: "Whence is this to me, that the mother of my Lord should come to me? For behold, that which is in me leaped and blessed thee." But Mary forgot the mysteries which the [arch]angel Gabriel had told her, and raised a sigh towards heaven and said: "Who am I, Lord, that all the women [generations] of the earth count me blessed?" 3. And she remained three months with Elizabeth. Day by day her womb grew, and Mary was afraid and went into her house and hid herself from the children of Israel. And Mary was sixteen years old when all these mysterious things happened.

13. 1. Now when she was in her sixth month, behold, Joseph came from his building and entered his house and found her with child. And he smote his face, threw himself down on sackcloth, and wept bitterly, saying: "With what countenance shall I look towards the Lord my God? What prayer shall I offer for her [for this maiden]? For I received her as a virgin out of the temple of the Lord my God and have not protected her. Who has deceived me? Who has done this evil in my house and defiled her [the virgin]? Has the story (of Adam) been repeated in me? For as Adam was (absent) in the hour of his prayer and the serpent came and found Eve alone and deceived her and defiled her, so also has it happened to me." 2. And Joseph arose from the sackcloth and called Mary and said to her: "You who are cared for by God, why have you done this and forgotten the Lord your God? Why have you humiliated your soul, you who were brought up in the Holy of Holies and received food from the hand of an angel?" 3. But she wept bitterly, saying: "I am pure, and know not a man." And Joseph said to her: "Whence then is this in your womb?" And she said: "As the Lord my God lives, I do not know whence it has come to me."

14. 1. And Joseph feared greatly and parted from her, pondering

what he should do with her. And Joseph said: "If I conceal her sin, I shall be found opposing the law of the Lord. If I expose her to the children of Israel, I fear lest that which is in her may have sprung from the angels and I should be found delivering up innocent blood to the judgment of death. What then shall I do with her? I will put her away secretly." And the night came upon him. 2. And behold, an angel of the Lord appeared to him in a dream, saying: "Do not fear because of this child. For that which is in her is of the Holy Spirit. She shall bear a son, and you shall call his name Jesus; for he shall save his people from their sins." And Joseph arose from sleep and glorified the God of Israel who had bestowed his grace upon him, and he watched over her.

15. 1. And Annas the scribe came to him and said to him: "Joseph, why did you not appear in our assembly?" And Joseph said to him: "I was weary from the journey, and I rested the first day." And Annas turned and saw that Mary was with child. 2. And he went hastily to the priest and said to him: "Joseph, for whom you are a witness, has grievously transgressed." And the high priest said: "In what way?" And he said: "The virgin, whom he received from the temple of the Lord, he has defiled, and has stolen marriage with her, and has not disclosed it to the children of Israel." And the high priest said to him: "Joseph! Joseph has done this?" And [Annas] said to him: "Send officers, and you will find the virgin with child." And the officers went and found her as he had said, and brought her to the temple. And she stood before the court. And the priest said: "Mary, why have you done this? Why have you humiliated your soul and forgotten the Lord your God, you who were brought up in the Holy of Holies, and received food from the hand of an angel, and heard hymns of praise, and danced before him? Why have you done this?" But she wept bitterly, saying: "As the Lord my God lives, I am pure before him and I know not a man." And the high priest said to Joseph: "Why have you done this?" And Joseph said: "As the Lord my God lives I am pure concerning her." And the high priest said: "Do not give false witness, but speak the truth. You have stolen marriage with her [consummated your marriage in secret], and have not disclosed it to the children of Israel, and have not bowed your head under the mighty hand in order that your seed might be blessed." And Joseph was silent.

16. 1. And the high priest said: "Give back the virgin whom you have received from the temple of the Lord." And Joseph wept bitterly. And the high priest said: "I will give you [both] to drink the water of the conviction of the Lord, and it will make manifest your sins before your

eyes." 2. And the high priest took (it) and gave (it) to Joseph to drink and sent him into the wilderness [into the hill-country]; and he came (back) whole. And he made Mary also drink, and sent her into the wilderness [into the hill-country]; and she (also) returned whole. And all the people marvelled, because (the water) had not revealed any sin in them. And the high priest said: "If the Lord God has not made manifest your sins, neither do I condemn you." And he released them. And Joseph took Mary and departed to his house, rejoicing and glorifying the God of Israel.

17. 1. Now there went out a decree from the king Augustus that all (inhabitants) of Bethlehem in Judaea should be enrolled. And Joseph said: "I shall enroll my sons, but what shall I do with this child? How shall I enroll her? As my wife? I am ashamed to do that. Or as my daughter? But all the children of Israel know that she is not my daughter. The day of the Lord himself will do as [t]he [Lord] wills." 2. And he saddled his ass [his she-ass] and sat her on it; his son led it, and Samuel [Joseph] followed. And they drew near to the third mile(stone). And Joseph turned round and saw her sad, and said within himself: "Perhaps that which is within her is paining her." And again Joseph turned round and saw her laughing. And he said to her: "Mary, why is it that I see your face at one time laughing and at another sad?" And she said to him: "Joseph, I see with my eyes two peoples, one weeping and lamenting and one rejoicing and exulting." 3. And they came half the way, and Mary said to him: "Joseph, take me down from the ass [from the she-ass], for the child within me presses me, to come forth." And he took her down there and said to her: "Where shall I take you and hide your shame? For the place is desert."

18. 1. And he found a cave there and brought her into it, and left her in the care of his sons and went out to seek for a Hebrew midwife in the region of Bethlehem. [2. Now I, Joseph, was walking, and (yet) I did not walk, and I looked up to the air and saw the air in amazement. And I looked up at the vault of heaven, and saw it standing still and the birds of the heaven motionless. And I looked at the earth, and saw a dish placed there and workmen lying round it, with their hands in the dish. But those who chewed did not chew, and those who lifted up anything lifted up nothing, and those who put something to their mouth put nothing (to their mouth), but all had their faces turned upwards. And behold, sheep were being driven and (yet) they did not come forward, but stood still; and the shepherd raised his hand to strike them with his staff, but his hand remained up. And I looked at the flow

of the river, and saw the mouths of the kids over it and they did not drink. And then all at once everything went on its course (again).]

19. 1. And he found one who was just coming down from the hill-country, and he took her with him, and said to the midwife: "Mary is betrothed to me; but she conceived of the Holy Spirit after she had been brought up in the temple of the Lord."

[1. And behold, a woman came down from the hill-country and said to me: "Man, where are you going?" And I said: "I seek a Hebrew midwife." And she answered me: "Are you from Israel?" And I said to her: "Yes." And she said: "And who is she who brings forth in the cave?" And I said: "My betrothed." And she said to me: "Is she not your wife?" And I said to her: "She is Mary, who was brought up in the temple of the Lord, and I received her by lot as my wife. And (yet) she is not my wife, but she has conceived of the Holy Spirit." And the midwife said to him: "Is this true?" And Joseph said to her: "Come and see."]

And the midwife went with him. 2. And he went to the place of the cave, and behold, a dark [bright] cloud overshadowed the cave. And the midwife said: "My soul is magnified to-day, for my eyes have seen wonderful things; for salvation is born to Israel." And immediately the cloud disappeared from the cave, and a great light appeared, so that our eyes could not bear it. A short time afterwards that light withdrew until the child appeared, and it went and took the breast of its mother Mary. And the midwife cried: "How great is this day to me, that I have seen this new sight." 3. And the midwife came out of the cave, and Salome met her. And she said to her: "Salome, Salome, I have a new sight to tell you; a virgin has brought forth, a thing which her nature does not allow." And Salome said: "As the Lord my God lives, unless I put (forward) my finger and test her condition, I will not believe that a virgin has brought forth."

20. 1. And Salome went in and made her ready

[1. And the midwife went in and said to Mary: "Make yourself ready, for there is no small con-

tention concerning you." And
Salome put (forward) her finger]

to test her condition. And she cried out, saying:

["Woe for my wickedness and my
unbelief; for]

"I have tempted the living God; and behold, my hand falls away from
me, consumed by fire!"

2. And she prayed to the Lord.   [2. And she bowed her knees
before the Lord, saying: "O God
of my fathers, remember me; for I
am the seed of Abraham, Isaac
and Jacob; do not make me a
public example to the children of
Israel, but restore me to the poor.
For thou knowest, Lord, that in
thy name I perform my duties and
from thee I have received my
hire."]

3. And behold, an angel of the Lord stood before Salome and said to
her: "The Lord God has heard your prayer. Come near, touch the
child, and you will be healed." 4. And she did so. [And she said: "I will
worship him, for (in him) a great king has been born to Israel."] And
Salome was healed as she had requested, and she went out of the cave
[justified]. And behold, an angel of the Lord [a voice] cried: "Salome,
Salome, tell [not] what marvel you have seen, before the child comes
to Jerusalem."

21. 1. And behold, Joseph prepared to go forth to Judaea. And there
took place a great tumult in Bethlehem of Judaea. For there came wise
men saying: "Where is the [new-born] king of the Jews? For we have
seen his star in the east and have come to worship him." 2. When
Herod heard this he was troubled and sent officers [to the wise men],

and sent for them and they told   [and sent for the high priests and
him about the star.   questioned them: "How is it written concerning the Messiah?
Where is he born?" They said to
him: "In Bethlehem of Judaea; for
so it is written." And he let them
go. And he questioned the wise

men and said to them: "What sign did you see concerning the new-born king?" And the wise men said: "We saw how an indescribably greater star shone among these stars and dimmed them, so that they no longer shone; and so we knew that a king was born for Israel. And we have come to worship him." And Herod said: "Go and seek, and when you have found him, tell me, that I also may come to worship him."

3. And behold, they saw stars [a star] in the east, and they [it] went before them,

3. And the wise men went forth. And behold, the star which they had seen in the east, went before them,]

until they came to the cave. And it stood over the head of the child [the cave]. And the wise men saw the young child with Mary his mother, and they took out of their bag gifts, gold, and frankincense and myrrh. 4. And being warned by the angel that they should not go into Judaea, they went to their own country by another way.

22. 1. But when Herod perceived that he had been tricked by the wise men he was angry and sent his murderers and commanded them to kill all the children who were two years old and under. 2. When Mary heard that the children were to be killed, she was afraid and took the child and wrapped him in swaddling clothes and laid him in an ox-manger.

3. But Elizabeth, when she heard that John was sought for, took him and went up into the hill-country. And she looked around (to see) where she could hide him, and there was no hiding-place. And Elizabeth groaned aloud and said: "O mountain of God, receive me, a mother, with my child." For Elizabeth could not go up (further) for fear. And immediately the mountain was rent asunder and received her. And that mountain made a light to gleam for her; for an angel of the Lord was with them and protected them.

23. 1. Now Herod was searching for John, and sent officers to Zacharias at the altar to ask him: "Where have you hidden your son?" And he answered and said to them: "I am a minister of God and attend continually upon his temple. How should I know where my son is?" 2.

And the officers departed and told all this to Herod. Then Herod was angry and said, "Is his son to be king over Israel?" And he sent the officers to him again with the command: "Tell the truth. Where is your son? You know that your blood is under my hand." And the officers departed and told him all this. 3. And Zacharias said: "I am a martyr of God. Take my blood! But my spirit the Lord will receive, for you shed innocent blood in the forecourt of the temple of the Lord." And about the dawning of the day Zacharias was slain. And the children of Israel did not know that he had been slain.

24. 1. Rather, at the hour of the salutation the priests were departing, but the blessing of Zacharias did not meet them according to custom. And the priests stood waiting for Zacharias, to greet him with prayer and to glorify the Most High. 2. But when he delayed to come, they were all afraid. But one of them took courage and went into the sanctuary. And he saw beside the altar congealed blood; and a voice said: "Zacharias has been slain, and his blood shall not be wiped away until his avenger comes." And when he heard these words, he was afraid, and went out and told the priests what he had seen. 3. And they heard and saw what had happened. And the panel-work of the ceiling of the temple wailed, and they rent their clothes from the top to the bottom. And they did not find his body, but they found his blood turned into stone. And they were afraid, and went out and told all the people: "Zacharias has been slain." And all the tribes of the people heard it and mourned him and lamented three days and three nights. 4. And after the three days the priests took counsel whom they should appoint in his stead. And the lot fell upon Symeon. Now it was he to whom it had been revealed by the Holy Spirit that he should not see death until he had seen the Christ in the flesh.

25. 1. Now I, James, who wrote this history, when a tumult arose in Jerusalem on the death of Herod, withdrew into the wilderness until the tumult in Jerusalem ceased. And I will praise the Lord, who gave me the wisdom to write this history. Grace shall be with all those who fear the Lord.

Nativity of Mary. Apocalypse of James. Peace be to him who wrote and to him who reads!

The Infancy Gospel of Thomas

The Infancy Gospel of Thomas (Inf. Thom.) *is a collection of novelistic miracle stories, purported to have been performed by Jesus prior to his twelfth birthday. The original language in which this gospel was written is not yet clear: either Greek or Syriac is possible. The oldest textual witness is a sixth century* C.E. *Syriac manuscript from the British Museum. The Greek text is extant in several manuscripts that date from the fourteenth to sixteenth centuries; these manuscripts have been arranged stemmatically into two recensions, of which the longer recension seems to preserve the better text. Numerous translations into ancient languages were also made in antiquity, reflecting the esteem with which this document was held in the church. The manuscript tradition gives several different titles to the work. Attribution of authorship to Thomas seems to be a secondary, late development. Identifying the provenance of the work is difficult, although a location in eastern Syria, where Thomas traditions had their origin, is most likely.*

Scholars have generally accepted the identification of the Infancy Gospel of Thomas *with an unnamed "apocryphal" writing which was used by the Marcosians (a group of Christian gnostics who were prominent in the second century) and cited by Ireneus (a church writer who lived at the end of the second century). In his citation, Ireneus first quotes a non-canonical story that circulated about the childhood of Jesus and then goes directly on to quote a passage from the infancy narrative of the Gospel of Luke (Luke 2:49). Since the* Infancy Gospel of Thomas *records both of these stories, in relatively close proximity to one another, it is possible that the apocryphal writing cited by Ireneus is, in fact, what is now known as the* Infancy Gospel of Thomas. *Because of the complexities of the manuscript tradition, however, there*

is no certainty as to when the stories of the Infancy Gospel of Thomas
began to be written down. Since the history of this document is that of
the fixing in writing of a cycle of oral tradition, one has to reckon with
the fact that the oral transmission of these folkloristic tales occurred not
only prior to but also simultaneous with the written transmission.
Stories circulated from the oral to the written tradition and back again
with relative fluidity.

The Infancy Gospel of Thomas carries forward the aretalogical
tradition of the gospels, expanding it to include an enumeration of
miraculous feats performed even while Jesus was a mere infant. The
social setting that gave rise to the production and transmission of these
miracle stories was Christian missionary propaganda, which endeav-
ored to legitimate the authority of Jesus among all other religious and
political leaders within the Greco-Roman world. In this respect, the
Infancy Gospel of Thomas can be profitably compared with the
legendary accounts made at that time of other "divine men" in
antiquity, both of great religious figures of the distant past (such as
Moses) and of political leaders of more contemporary times (such as
Alexander the Great and Caesar Augustus). The impetus of this
particular tradition was the cataloging of the miraculous works of the
young hero. It was characteristic of these legends that the first public
words and deeds of the hero were thought to be indicative of his status
and future career. Accordingly, the Infancy Gospel of Thomas lays
stress upon what it understood to be Jesus' self-awareness, wisdom,
divine identity, and destiny.

The sources of the Infancy Gospel of Thomas are oral traditions and
the Gospel of Luke; these have been laced with a keen, lively sense of
imagination. Jesus is depicted as an enfant terrible, always clever and
mischievous, often intractable and even malicious. The biographic
legends of Jesus, at school and at play, display nothing distinctively
Christian at all: Jesus is portrayed simply as a child of the gods, a
Wunderkind in whose life are manifested epiphanies of the divine.
Ironically, the descriptions of the precocious glee of the infant Jesus both
hint at his humanity and detract from it as well. These stories
adumbrate the tyranny of the miracle tradition.

The Gospels of Matthew and Luke also attest to an interest in the
infancy of Jesus. Luke's incorporation into his gospel of the story of the
boy Jesus in the Temple (Luke 2:41–52) bears witness to an early
preoccupation with the "hidden life" of Jesus, and demonstrates that he
knew of other such legends in circulation. The Infancy Gospel of
Thomas has appropriated this story from Luke, retaining the language,

structure, and distinctively Lucan redactional features in the narrative, including Luke's portrayal of Jesus as a "divine man" and polemical interest in Jesus' own knowledge of his mission. The climax of the story, however, has been transformed to fit the theological program of the entire Infancy Gospel of Thomas: the portrayal of the works and wisdom of Jesus, the magician.

The Infancy Gospel of Thomas has been influential in the continuing development of infancy narratives of Jesus, being used as a source for infancy gospels which were composed not only in the early Middle Ages but even in modern times. Whereas Matthew and Luke bear witness to the merging of these aretalogical traditions into the generic pattern of the Gospel of Mark, the Infancy Gospel of Thomas demonstrates both the fecundity of these traditions and their adaptability in the expanding trajectory of gospel literature. Its date of composition is sometime after that of its written source, the Gospel of Luke, and before the oldest textual witness in the sixth century. If Ireneus' citation is judged to be an attestation of at least portions of the written text, then a date of composition of an edition of the Infancy Gospel of Thomas in the mid- to late second century would be most plausible.

The text is numbered according to chapter and verse divisions (1.1– 19.5). The translation was made by Oscar Cullmann and A. J. B. Higgins (New Testament Apocrypha).

The Infancy Gospel of Thomas

The Account of Thomas the Israelite Philosopher concerning the Childhood of the Lord

1. 1. I, Thomas the Israelite, tell and make known to you all, brethren from among the Gentiles, all the works of the childhood of our Lord Jesus Christ and his mighty deeds, which he did when he was born in our land. The beginning is as follows.

2. 1. When this boy Jesus was five years old he was playing at the ford of a brook, and he gathered together into pools the water that flowed by, and made it at once clean, and commanded it by his word alone. 2. He made soft clay and fashioned from it twelve sparrows. And it was the sabbath when he did this. And there were also many other children playing with him. 3. Now when a certain Jew saw what Jesus was doing in his play on the sabbath, he at once went and told his father Joseph: "See, your child is at the brook, and he has taken clay and fashioned twelve birds and has profaned the sabbath." 4. And when Joseph came to the place and saw (it), he cried out to him, saying: "Why do you do on the sabbath what ought not to be done?" But Jesus clapped his hands and cried to the sparrows: "Off with you!" And the sparrows took flight and went away chirping. 5. The Jews were amazed when they saw this, and went away and told their elders what they had seen Jesus do.

3. 1. But the son of Annas the scribe was standing there with Joseph; and he took a branch of a willow and (with it) dispersed the water which Jesus had gathered together. 2. When Jesus saw what he had done he was enraged and said to him: "You insolent, godless dunderhead, what harm did the pools and the water do to you? See, now you also shall wither like a tree and shall bear neither leaves nor root nor fruit." 3. And immediately that lad withered up completely; and Jesus departed and went into Joseph's house. But the parents of him that was withered took him away, bewailing his youth, and brought him to Joseph and reproached him: "What a child you have, who does such things."

4. 1. After this again he went through the village, and a lad ran and knocked against his shoulder. Jesus was exasperated and said to him: "You shall not go further on your way," and the child immediately fell down and died. But some, who saw what took place, said: "From where does this child spring, since his every word is an accomplished deed?" 2. And the parents of the dead child came to Joseph and blamed him and said: "Since you have such a child, you cannot dwell with us in the village; or else teach him to bless and not to curse. For he is slaying our children."

5. 1. And Joseph called the child aside and admonished him saying: "Why do you do such things that these people (must) suffer and hate us and persecute us?" But Jesus replied: "I know that these words are not yours; nevertheless for your sake I will be silent. But they shall bear their punishment." And immediately those who had accused him became blind. 2. And those who saw it were greatly afraid and perplexed, and said concerning him: "Every word he speaks, whether good or evil, was a deed and became a marvel." And when Joseph saw that Jesus had so done, he arose and took him by the ear and pulled it hard. 3. And the child was angry and said to him: "It is sufficient for

you to seek and not to find, and most unwisely have you acted. Do you
not know that I am yours? Do not vex me."

6. 1. Now a certain teacher, Zacchaeus by name, who was standing
there, heard in part Jesus saying these things to his father, and
marvelled greatly that, being a child, he said such things. 2. And after
a few days he came near to Joseph and said to him: "You have a clever
child, and he has understanding. Come, hand him over to me that he
may learn letters, and I will teach him with the letters all knowledge,
and to salute all the older people and honour them as grandfathers and
fathers, and to love those of his own age." 3. And he told him all the
letters from Alpha to Omega clearly, with much questioning. But he
looked at Zacchaeus the teacher and said to him: "How do you, who
do not know the Alpha according to its nature, teach others the Beta?
Hypocrite, first if you know it, teach the Alpha, and then we shall
believe you concerning the Beta." Then he began to question the
teacher about the first letter, and he was unable to answer him. 4. And
in the hearing of many the child said to Zacchaeus: "Hear, teacher,
the arrangement of the first letter, and pay heed to this, how it has lines
and a middle mark which goes through the pair of lines which you see,
(how these lines) converge, rise, turn in the dance, three signs of the
same kind, subject to and supporting one another, of equal propor-
tions; here you have the lines of the Alpha."

7. 1. Now when Zacchaeus the teacher heard so many such
allegorical descriptions of the first letter being expounded, he was
perplexed at such a reply and such great teaching and said to those who
were present: "Woe is me, I am forced into a quandary, wretch that I
am; I have brought shame to myself in drawing to myself this child. 2.
Take him away, therefore, I beseech you, brother Joseph. I cannot
endure the severity of his look, I cannot make out his speech at all.
This child is not earth-born; he can tame even fire. Perhaps he was
begotten even before the creation of the world. What belly bore him,
what womb nurtured him I do not know. Woe is me, my friend, he
stupefies me, I cannot follow his understanding. I have deceived
myself, thrice wretched man that I am. I strove to get a disciple, and
have found myself with a teacher. 3. My friends, I think of my shame,
that I, an old man, have been overcome by a child. I can only despair
and die because of this child, for I cannot in this hour look him in the
face. And when all say that I have been overcome by a small child,
what have I to say? And what can I tell concerning the lines of the first
letter of which he spoke to me? I do not know, my friends, for I know
neither beginning nor end of it. 4. Therefore I ask you, brother Joseph,

take him away to your house. He is something great, a god or an angel
or what I should say I do not know."

8. 1. And while the Jews were trying to console Zacchaeus, the
child laughed aloud and said: "Now let that which is yours bear fruit,
and let the blind in heart see. I have come from above to curse them
and call them to the things above, as he commanded who sent me for
your sakes." 2. And when the child had ceased speaking, immediately
all those were healed who had fallen under his curse. And no one after
that dared to provoke him, lest he should curse him, and he should be
maimed.

9. 1. Now after some days Jesus was playing in the upper story of a
house, and one of the children who were playing with him fell down
from the house and died. And when the other children saw it they fled,
and Jesus remained alone. 2. And the parents of him that was dead
came and accused him of having thrown him down. And Jesus replied:
"I did not throw him down." But they continued to revile him. 3.
Then Jesus leaped down from the roof and stood by the body of the
child, and cried with a loud voice: "Zenon"—for that was his name—
"arise and tell me, did I throw you down?" And he arose at once and
said: "No, Lord, you did not throw me down, but raised me up." And
when they saw it they were amazed. And the parents of the child
glorified God for the miracle that had happened and worshipped Jesus.

10. 1. After a few days a young man was cleaving wood in a corner,
and the axe fell and split the sole of his foot, and he bled so much that
he was about to die. 2. And when a clamour arose and a concourse of
people took place, the child Jesus also ran there, and forced his way
through the crowd, and took the injured foot, and it was healed
immediately. And he said to the young man: "Arise now, cleave the
wood and remember me." And when the crowd saw what happened,
they worshipped the child, saying: "Truly the spirit of God dwells in
this child."

11. 1. When he was six years old, his mother gave him a pitcher
and sent him to draw water and bring it into the house. 2. But in the
crowd he stumbled, and the pitcher was broken. But Jesus spread out
the garment he was wearing, filled it with water and brought it to his
mother. And when his mother saw the miracle, she kissed him, and
kept within herself the mysteries which she had seen him do.

12. 1. Again, in the time of sowing the child went out with his
father to sow wheat in their land. And as his father sowed, the child
Jesus also sowed one corn of wheat. 2. And when he had reaped it and
threshed it, he brought in a hundred measures; and he called all the

poor of the village to the threshing-floor and gave them the wheat, and Joseph took the residue of the wheat. He was eight years old when he worked this miracle.

13. 1. His father was a carpenter and made at that time ploughs and yokes. And he received an order from a rich man to make a bed for him. But when one beam was shorter than its corresponding one and they did not know what to do, the child Jesus said to his father Joseph: "Put down the two pieces of wood and make them even from the middle to one end." 2. And Joseph did as the child told him. And Jesus stood at the other end and took hold of the shorter piece of wood, and stretching it made it equal with the other. And his father Joseph saw it and was amazed, and he embraced the child and kissed him, saying: "Happy am I that God has given me this child."

14. 1. And when Joseph saw the understanding of the child and his age, that he was growing to maturity, he resolved again that he should not remain ignorant of letters; and he took him and handed him over to another teacher. And the teacher said to Joseph: "First I will teach him Greek, and then Hebrew." For the teacher knew the child's knowledge and was afraid of him. Nevertheless he wrote the alphabet and practised it with him for a long time; but he gave him no answer. 2. And Jesus said to him: "If you are indeed a teacher, and if you know the letters well, tell me the meaning of the Alpha, and I will tell you that of the Beta." And the teacher was annoyed and struck him on the head. And the child was hurt and cursed him, and he immediately fainted and fell to the ground on his face. 3. And the child returned to Joseph's house. But Joseph was grieved and commanded his mother: "Do not let him go outside the door, for all those who provoke him die."

15. 1. And after some time yet another teacher, a good friend of Joseph, said to him: "Bring the child to me to the school. Perhaps I by persuasion can teach him the letters." And Joseph said to him: "If you have the courage, brother, take him with you." And he took him with fear and anxiety, but the child went gladly. 2. And he went boldly into the school and found a book lying on the reading-desk and took it, but did not read the letters in it, but opened his mouth and spoke by the Holy Spirit and taught the law to those that stood by. And a large crowd assembled and stood there listening to him, wondering at the grace of his teaching and the readiness of his words, that although an infant he made such utterances. 3. But when Joseph heard it, he was afraid and ran to the school, wondering whether this teacher also was without skill (maimed). But the teacher said to Joseph: "Know,

brother, that I took the child as a disciple; but he is full of great grace
and wisdom; and now I beg you, brother, take him to your house." 4.
And when the child heard this, he at once smiled on him and said:
"Since you have spoken well and have testified rightly, for your sake
shall he also that was smitten be healed." And immediately the other
teacher was healed. And Joseph took the child and went away to his
house.

16. 1. Joseph sent his son James to bind wood and take it into his
house, and the child Jesus followed him. And while James was
gathering the sticks, a viper bit the hand of James. 2. And as he lay
stretched out and about to die, Jesus came near and breathed upon the
bite, and immediately the pain ceased, and the creature burst, and at
once James became well.

17. 1. And after these things in the neighbourhood of Joseph a
little sick child died, and his mother wept bitterly. And Jesus heard that
great mourning and tumult arose, and he ran quickly, and finding the
child dead, he touched his breast and said: "I say to you, do not die but
live and be with your mother." And immediately it looked up and
laughed. And he said to the woman: "Take him and give him milk and
remember me." 2. And when the people standing round saw it, they
marvelled and said: "Truly, this child is either a god or an angel of
God, for every word of his is an accomplished deed." And Jesus
departed from there and played with other children.

18. 1. After some time a house was being built and a great
disturbance arose, and Jesus arose and went there. And seeing a man
lying dead he took his hand and said: "I say to you, man, arise, do your
work." And immediately he arose and worshipped him. 2. And when
the people saw it, they were amazed and said: "This child is from
heaven, for he has saved many souls from death, and is able to save
them all his life long."

19. 1. And when he was twelve years old his parents went
according to the custom to Jerusalem to the feast of the passover with
their company, and after the passover they returned to go to their
house. And while they were returning the child Jesus went back to
Jerusalem. But his parents supposed that he was in the company. 2.
And when they had gone a day's journey, they sought him among their
kinsfolk, and when they did not find him, they were troubled, and
returned again to the city seeking him. And after the third day they
found him in the temple sitting among the teachers, listening to the
law and asking them questions. And all paid attention to him and
marvelled how he, a child, put to silence the elders and teachers of the

people, expounding the sections of the law and the sayings of the prophets. 3. And his mother Mary came near and said to him: "Why have you done this to us, child? Behold, we have sought you sorrowing." Jesus said to them: "Why do you seek me? Do you not know that I must be in my Father's house?" 4. But the scribes and Pharisees said: "Are you the mother of this child?" And she said: "I am." And they said to her: "Blessed are you among women, because the Lord has blessed the fruit of your womb. For such glory and such excellence and wisdom we have never seen nor heard." 5. And Jesus arose and followed his mother and was subject to his parents; but his mother kept (in her heart) all that had taken place. And Jesus increased in wisdom and stature and grace. To him be glory for ever and ever. Amen.

The Epistula Apostolorum

The Epistula Apostolorum (Ep. Apost.) *is a document of Christian polemics that presents, in the form of an alleged revelation of Jesus to his apostles, the position of a group of emerging "catholic" Christians in opposition to that ascribed to their opponents in the church. Through this revelation the "catholics" seek to legitimate their own interpretation of the Christian traditions. This document begins with an epistolary introduction, purporting to be a letter sent by all the apostles to the churches of the world, in which followers of the teachings of Simon and Cerinthus (alleged leaders of groups of Christian gnostics who were prominent throughout the second century) are opposed.*

Originally written in Greek, the Epistula Apostolorum *is extant in Coptic and Ethiopic translations. The Coptic is the oldest and most important textual witness, being a translation directly from the original Greek. It is preserved in a fragmentary papyrus that dates from the late fourth or early fifth century* C.E. *This manuscript was discovered in 1895, first published in 1919, and is housed in the Institut de la Mission Archéologique Française in Cairo. The Ethiopic is the only translation that preserves the complete text of the* Epistula Apostolorum. *Extant in several late manuscripts, of which the most important is an eighteenth-century text now in the British Museum, the Ethiopic seems to be a translation of an Arabic version of either the original Greek or another Coptic translation of the Greek. The title of the* Epistula Apostolorum *has not been transmitted from antiquity, but may be inferred from its opening, which refers to itself as "the letter of the council of the apostles."*

In presenting an alleged revelation of Jesus to his apostles, the Epistula Apostolorum *superimposes the literary form of revelation* discourse and dialogue upon its traditions. Jesus speaks as the risen Lord who mediates instruction to the community. This literary layering is clearly secondary: the discourse and dialogue are not composed of sayings, but comprise creedal formulas, catechetical instructions, and portions of abbreviated dogmatic treatises, all of which are used in the service of "orthodoxy." The Epistula Apostolorum thus mimics a form of revelation literature which was popular among many gnostics, attempting to combat its opponents with their own theological weapons. This apologetic purpose is heightened by prefixing an epistolary introduction to the document. Against the claims of authority of certain writings that circulated under the names of individual apostles or disciples of Jesus, all the apostles are mentioned by name as the authors of this "letter" and the recipients of this revelation. The Epistula Apostolorum thus modifies the form of the letter to stress that this revelation is encompassed within a truly catholic epistle, that it is not a secret teaching, and that what is revealed is known by and available to all. The Epistula Apostolorum, therefore, is an anti-genre, a parody of a form of apocalyptic literature favored by its Christian gnostic opponents, an attempt to domesticate the literature of those who portrayed Jesus as the revealer of otherworldly knowledge disclosed in mystery books.

The apologetic intent of the Epistula Apostolorum is in evidence in its presentation of Jesus traditions. The account of Jesus' appearance to the disciples, which introduces the revelation discourse, emphasizes the physical reality of the resurrection. This account, moreover, is not built upon discrete sayings but upon the narrative material of the gospel traditions. This narrative seems to be constructed in part from the resurrection stories of the gospels of the New Testament. These gospels are considered authoritative, but the stories are referred to quite freely, without a formula of introduction which would normally be used to indicate "scriptural" status. Here, too, doctrinal discourse has supplanted the more primitive traditions of sayings and deeds of Jesus.

An important source of the traditions of the Epistula Apostolorum is a Christian creed. References to Jesus' deeds, based in part upon the gospels of the New Testament, but also upon an infancy gospel, are interspersed throughout the explication of the various articles of the creed. This creed seems to be a major structuring principle in the composition of the document. Its close parallels with the creed found in the writings of Justin (a church apologist who lived in the middle of the second century) suggest that the Epistula Apostolorum may be indica-

tive of the state of affairs at the time of Justin, bearing witness to the development and deployment of the creed in the church. Moreover, just as the interpretation of the appearance stories seeks to confirm the physical reality of the resurrection of Jesus, so also the exposition of the creedal tradition is seen to be validated by references to the "historical" documents of the earthly life of Jesus. Gospel literature has thereby been transformed from the diverse reflections of believers who produced sayings of and stories about Jesus into a fixed written tradition, containing putatively verifying historical information, serving as an alleged authentic repository of records of events that legitimate the beliefs of one particular group of Christians.

The Epistula Apostolorum *was composed sometime after the gospels of the New Testament and before the Coptic translation was made in the fourth or fifth century. The freedom in its use of traditions, the adaptation of the gospels into regulations for church order, the way in which the creed's position is consolidated and used to combat its gnostic opponents, and the co-opting of the apostle Paul as a subordinate of the emerging "catholic" church—all of this suggests that this document was composed in the mid- to late second century. Internal evidence suggests that Egypt was its place of origin.*

When the Coptic and Ethiopic versions of the text differ significantly from one another, these differences are noted by printing the reading of one text or the other in parentheses, with a reference to the respective version given in italics. When these divergent readings are extensive, the text is printed in parallel columns, with the Ethiopic on the left-hand side and the Coptic on the right-hand side of the page.

The text is numbered according to chapter divisions (1–51). The translation was made by Hugo Duensing and Richard E. Taylor (New Testament Apocrypha).

The Epistula Apostolorum

1. *(Chapters 1–6 in Ethiopic only.)* What Jesus Christ revealed to his disciples as a letter, and how Jesus Christ revealed the letter of the council of the apostles, the disciples of Jesus Christ, to the Catholics;

which was written because of the false apostles Simon and Cerinthus, that no one should follow them—for in them is deceit with which they kill men—that you may be established and not waver, not be shaken and not turn away from the word of the Gospel that you have heard. As we have heard (it), kept (it), and have written (it) for the whole world, so we entrust (it) to you, our sons and daughters, in joy and in the name of God the Father, the ruler of the world, and in Jesus Christ. May Grace increase upon you.

2. (We,) John and Thomas and Peter and Andrew and James and Philip and Bartholomew and Matthew and Nathanael and Judas Zelotes and Cephas, we have written (or: write) to the churches of the East and West, towards North and South, recounting and proclaiming to you concerning our Lord Jesus Christ, how we have written and heard and felt him after he had risen from the dead, and how he has revealed to us things great, astonishing, real.

3. We know this: our Lord and Savior Jesus Christ (is) God, Son of God who was sent from God, the ruler of the entire world, the maker and creator of what is named with every name, who is over all authority (as) Lord of lords and King of kings, the ruler of the rulers, the heavenly one who is over the Cherubim and Seraphim and sits at the right hand of the throne of the Father, who by his word commanded the heavens and built the earth and all that is in it and bounded the sea that it should not go beyond its boundaries, and (caused) deeps and springs to bubble up and flow over the earth day and night; who established the sun, moon, and stars in heaven and separated light from darkness; who commanded hell, and in the twinkling of an eye summons the rain for the wintertime, and fog, frost, and hail, and the days (?) in their time; who shakes and makes firm; who has created man according to his image and likeness; who spoke in parables through the patriarchs and prophets and in truth through him whom the apostles declared and the disciples touched. And God, the Lord, the Son of God—we believe that the word, which became flesh through the holy virgin Mary, was carried (conceived) in her womb by the Holy Spirit, and was born not by the lust of the flesh but by the will of God, and was wrapped (in swaddling clothes) and made known at Bethlehem; and that he was reared and grew up, as we saw.

4. This is what our Lord Jesus Christ did, who was delivered by Joseph and Mary his mother to where he might learn letters. And he who taught him said to him as he taught him, "Say Alpha." He

answered and said to him, "First you tell me what Beta is." And . . .
true . . . a real thing which was done.

5. Then there was a marriage in Cana of Galilee. And he was
invited with his mother and his brothers. And he made water into wine
and awakened the dead and made the lame to walk; for him whose
hand was withered, he stretched it out again, and the woman who
suffered twelve years from a haemorrhage touched the edge of his
garment and was immediately whole; and while we reflected and
wondered concerning the miracle he performed, he said to us, "Who
touched me?" And we said to him, "O Lord, the crowd of people
touched you." And he answered and said to us, "I noticed that a power
went out from me." Immediately that woman came before him,
answered him and said to him, "Lord, I touched you." And he
answered and said to her, "Go, your faith has made you whole." Then
he made the deaf to hear and the blind to see, and he exorcized those
who were possessed, and he cleansed the lepers. And the demon
Legion, that a man had, met with Jesus, cried and said, "Before the
day of our destruction has come You have come to turn us out." But
the Lord Jesus rebuked him and said to him, "Go out of this man
without doing anything to him." And he went into the swine and
drowned them in the sea, and they were choked. Then he walked on
the sea, and the winds blew, and he rebuked them, and the waves of
the sea became calm. And when we, his disciples, had no denarii, we
said to him, "Master, what should we do about the tax-collector?" And
he answered and said to us, "One of you cast the hook, the net, into
the deep and draw out a fish, and he will find a denarius in it. Give
that to the tax-collector for me and for you." Then when we had no
bread except five loaves and two fish, he commanded the people to lie
down, and their number amounted to 5000 besides children and
women, whom we served with pieces of bread; and they were filled,
and there was (some) left over, and we carried away twelve baskets full
of pieces, asking and saying, "What meaning is there in these five
loaves?" They are a picture of our faith concerning the great Christianity; and i.e. in the Father, the ruler of the entire world, and in Jesus
Christ our Savior, and in the Holy Spirit, the Paraclete, and in the
holy Church and in the forgiveness of sins.

6. And these things our Lord and Savior revealed and showed to us,
and likewise we to you, that you, reflecting upon eternal life, may
be associates in the grace of the Lord and in our service and in our
glory. Be firm, without wavering, in the knowledge and investigation

of our Lord Jesus Christ, and he will prove gracious and will save always and in all never ending eternity.

7. *(Here begins the Coptic.)* Cerinthus and Simon have come to go through the world. But they are the enemies of our Lord Jesus Christ,

who in reality alienate those who believe in the true word and deed, i.e. Jesus Christ. Therefore take care and beware of them, for in them is affliction and contamination and death, the end of which will be destruction and judgment.

for they pervert the words and the object, i.e. Jesus Christ. Now keep [yourselves] away from them, for death is in them and a great stain of corruption—these to whom shall be judgment and the end and eternal perdition.

8. Because of that we have not hesitated

with the true testimony of our Lord and Savior Jesus Christ, how he acted while we saw him, and how he constantly both explained and caused our thoughts within us.

to write to you concerning the testimony of our Savior Christ, what he did when we were behind him watching [and yet(?)] again in thoughts and deeds,

9. He of whom we are witnesses we know as the one crucified in the days of Pontius Pilate and of the prince Archelaus, who was crucified between two thieves, and was taken down from the wood of the cross together with them, and was buried in the place called qarānejō, to which three women came, Sarah, Martha, and Mary Magdalene. They carried ointment to pour out

he concerning whom [we] bear witness that the Lord is he who was crucified by Pontius Pilate and Archelaus between the two thieves

[and] who was buried in a place called the [place of the skull]. There went to that place [three] women: Mary, she who belonged to Martha, and Mary [Magd]alene. They took ointment to pour

upon his body, weeping and mourning over what had happened.

And they approached the tomb and found the stone where it had been rolled away from the tomb, and they opened the door

But when they had approached the tomb they looked inside

and did not find his (*Coptic:* the) body.

10. And (*Coptic:* But) as they were mourning and weeping, the Lord appeared to them and said to them, "(*Coptic:* For whom are you weeping? Now) do not weep; I am he whom you seek. But let one of you go to your brothers and say (*Ethiopic:* to them), 'Come, our (*Coptic:* the) Master has risen from the dead.' "

And Mary came to us and told us. And we said to her, "What have we to do with you, O woman? He that is dead and buried, can he then live?" And we did not believe her, that our Savior had risen from the dead.	Martha came and told it to us. We said to her, "What do you want with us, O woman? He who has died is buried, and could it be possible for him to live?" We did not believe her, that the Savior had risen from the dead.

Then she went back to our (*Coptic:* the) Lord and said to him, "None of them believed me

concerning your resurrection." And he said to her,	that you are alive." He said,

"Let another one of you go (*Coptic:* to them) saying this again to them."

And Sarah came and gave us the same news, and we accused her of lying. And she returned to our Lord and spoke to him as Mary had.	Mary came and told us again, and we did not believe her. She returned to the Lord and she also told it to him.

11. Then (*Ethiopic:* And then) the Lord said to Mary and (*Coptic:* and also) to her sisters, "Let us go to them." And he came and found us inside, veiled.

And we doubted and did not believe. He came before us like a ghost and we did not believe that it was he. But it was he. And thus he said to us, "Come, and	He called us out. But we thought it was a ghost, and we did not believe it was the Lord. Then [he said] to us, "Come,

do not be afraid. I am your teacher (*Coptic:* [master]) whom you, Peter, denied three times (*Ethiopic:* before the cock crowed); and now do you deny again?"

And we went to him, thinking and doubting whether it was he. And he said to us,

But we went to him, doubting in [our] hearts whether it was possibly he. Then he said to [us],

"Why do you (Coptic: still) doubt and (Ethiopic: why) are you not believing? (Ethiopic: believing that) I am he who spoke to you concerning my flesh, my death, and my resurrection.

And that you may know that it is I, lay your hand, Peter, (and your finger) in the nailprint of my hands; and you, Thomas, in my side; and also you, Andrew, see whether my foot steps on the ground and leaves a footprint.

That you may know that it is I, put your finger, Peter, in the nailprints of my hands; and you, Thomas, put your finger in the spear-wounds of my side; but you, Andrew, look at my feet and see if they do not touch the ground.

For it is written in the prophet,

'But a ghost, a demon, leaves no print on the ground.' "

'The foot of a ghost or a demon does not join to the ground.' "

12. But now we felt him, that he had truly risen in the flesh. And then we fell on our faces before him, asked him for pardon and entreated him because we had not believed him. Then our Lord and Savior said to us, "Stand up and I will reveal to you what is on earth, and what is above heaven, and your resurrection that is in the kingdom of heaven, concerning which my Father has sent me, that I may take up you and those who believe in me."

But we [touched] him that we might truly know whether he [had risen] in the flesh, and we fell on our [faces] confessing our sin, that we had been [un]believing. Then the Lord our redeemer said, "Rise up, and I will reveal to you what is above heaven and what is in heaven, and your rest that is in the kingdom of heaven. For my [Father] has given me the power to take up you and those who believe in me."

13. And what he revealed is this, as he said to us, "While I was coming from the Father of all, passing by the heavens, wherein I put on the wisdom of the Father and by his power clothed myself in his power, I was

But what he revealed is this that he said, "But it happened, as I was about to come down from the Father of all, I passed by the heavens; I put on the wisdom of the Father and the power of his might (?). I was in the heavens, in the heavens. And passing by the angels and archangels in their form and as one of them, I passed by the orders, dominions, and princes, possessing the measure of the wisdom of the Father who sent me. And the archangels Michael and Gabriel, Raphael and Uriel followed me until the fifth firmament of heaven, while I appeared as one of them. This kind of power was given me by the Father. Then I made the archangels to become distracted with the voice and go up to the altar of the Father and serve the Father in his work until I should return to him. I did this thus in the likeness (or: form?) of his wisdom. For I became all in all with them, that I, having . . . the will of the mercy of the Father and perfected the glory of him who sent me, might return to him.

14. Do you know that the angel Gabriel came and brought the message to Mary?" And we said to him, "Yes, O Lord." And he answered and said to us, "Do you not remember that I previously said to you that I became like an angel to the angels?" And we said to him, "Yes, O Lord." And he said to us, "At that time I appeared in the form of the archangel Gabriel to (the virgin) Mary and spoke with her, and her heart received (me); she believed and laughed; and I, the Word, went

and I passed by the angels and archangels in their form, as if I were one of them among the dominions and powers. I passed through them, possessing the wisdom of him who sent me. But the chief leader of the angels is Michael, and Gabriel and Uriel and Raphael, but they followed me to the fifth firmament, thinking in their hearts that I was one of them. But the Father gave me power of this nature. And in that day I adorned the archangels with a wondrous voice that they might go up to the altar of the Father and serve and complete the service until I should go to him. Thus I did it through the wisdom of the likeness. For I became all things in everything that I might . . . the plan of the Father and perfect the glory of him who sent me, and might go to him.

For you know that the angel Gabriel brought the message to Mary." We answered, "Yes, O Lord." Then he answered and said to us, "Do you not then remember that a little while ago I told you I became an angel among angels and I became all things in everything?" We [said] to him, "Yes, O Lord." Then he answered and said to us, "On that day, when I took the form of the angel Gabriel, I appeared to Mary and [spoke] with her. Her heart received me and she believed; I

into her and became flesh; and I myself was servant for myself, and in the form of the image of an angel; so I will do after I have gone to my Father.

formed myself and entered into her womb; I became flesh, for I alone was servant to myself with respect to Mary in an appearance of the form of an angel. So will I do, after I have gone to the Father.

15. And you therefore celebrate the remembrance of my death, i.e. the passover;

And you remember my death. If now the passover takes place,

then will one of you (*Ethiopic:* who stands beside me) be thrown into prison for my name's sake, and he will

be very grieved and sorrowful, for while you celebrate the passover he who is in custody did not celebrate it with you. And I will send my power in the form of my angel, and the door of the prison will open, and he will come out and come to you to watch with you and to rest. And when you complete my Agape and my remembrance at the crowing of the cock, he will again be taken and thrown in prison for a testimony, until he comes out to preach, as I have commanded you." And we said to him, "O Lord, have you then not completed the drinking of the passover? Must we, then, do it again?" And he said to us, "Yes, until I come from the Father with my wounds."

[be] in sorrow and care that you celebrate [the] passover while he is in prison and [far] from you; for he will sorrow that he does not celebrate the passover [with] you. I will send my power in the [form] of the angel Gabriel, and the doors of the prison will be opened. He will go out and come to you; he will spend a night of the watch with [you] and stay with you until the cock crows. But when you complete the remembrance that is for me, and the Agape, he will again be thrown into prison for a testimony, until he comes out from there and preaches what I have delivered to you." And we said to him, "O Lord, is it perhaps necessary again that we take the cup and drink?" He said to us, "Yes, it is necessary until the day when I come with those who were killed for my sake."

16. And we said to him, "O Lord, great is this that you say and

We said to him, "O Lord, what you have revealed to us before-

reveal to us. In what kind of power and form are you about to come?" And he said to us, "Truly I say to you, I will come as the sun which bursts forth; thus will I, shining seven times brighter than it in glory, while I am carried on the wings of the clouds in splendour with my cross going on before me, come to the earth to judge the living and the dead."

17. And we said to him, "O Lord, how many years yet?" And he said to us, "When the hundred and fiftieth year is completed, between Pentecost and Passover will the coming of my Father take place." And we said to him, "O Lord, now you said to us, 'I will come,' and then you said, 'He who sent me will come.'" And he said to us, "I am wholly in the Father and the Father in me." Then we said to him, "Will you really leave us until your coming? Where will we find a teacher?" And he answered and said to us, "Do you not know that until now I am both here and there with him who sent me?" And we said to him, "O Lord, is it possible that you should be both here and there?" And he said to us, "I am wholly in the Father and the Father in me after his image and after his form and after his power and after his perfection and after his light, and I am his perfect word."

18. This is, when he was crucified, had died and risen again,

hand is great. In a power of what sort or in an appearance of what order will you come?" But he answered, saying, "Truly I say to you, I will come as does the sun that shines, and shining seven times brighter than it in my brightness; with the wings of the clouds [carry]ing me in splendour and the sign of the cross before me, I will come down to the earth to judge the living and the dead." But we said to him, "O Lord, after how many years yet will this happen?" He said to us, "When the hundredth part and the twentieth part is completed, between Pentecost and the feast of unleavened bread, will the coming of the Father take place." But we said to him, "Here now, what have you said to us, 'I will come,' and how do you say, 'It is he who sent me who will come'? " Then he said to us, "I am wholly in my Father and my Father is in me

with regard to the resemblance of form and of power (?) and of perfection and of light and of full measure and with regard to voice. I am the word.
I have become to him a thing, i.e. . . . . completed according to

as he said this, and the work that was thus accomplished in the flesh, that he was crucified, and his ascension—this is the fulfilling of the number. "And the wonders and his image and everything perfect you will see in me with respect to redemption which takes place through me, and while I go to the Father and into heaven. But look, a new commandment I give you, that you love one another the type; I have come into being on the eight(h day) which is the day of the Lord. But the whole completion of the completion you will see through the redemption that has happened to me, and you will see me, how I shall go to heaven to my Father who is in heaven. But look now, I give you a new commandment; love one another and . . . (*One leaf missing in the Coptic.*)

and obey each other and (that) continual peace reign among you. Love your enemies, and what you do not want done to you, that do to no one else.

19. And both preach and teach this to those who believe in me, and preach concerning the kingdom of my Father, and as my Father has given me the power so I give it to you that you may bring near the children of the heavenly father. Preach, and they will believe. You (it is) whose duty is to lead his children into heaven." And we said to him, "O Lord, it is possible for you to do what you have told us; but how will we be able to do (it)?" And he said to us, "Truly I say to you, preach and teach, as I will be with you. For I am well pleased to be with you, that you may become joint heirs with me of the kingdom of heaven of him who sent me. Truly I say to you, you will be my brothers and companions, for my Father has delighted in you and in those who will believe in me through you. Truly I say to you, such and so great a joy has my Father prepared (for you) that angels and powers desired and will desire to view and to see it, but they will not be allowed to see the greatness of my Father." And we said to him, "O Lord, what kind (of thing) is this that you tell us?"

And he said to us, "You will see a light brighter than light and more perfect than perfection. And the Son will be perfected through the Father, the light—for the Father is perfect—(the Son) whom death and resurrection make perfect, and the one accomplishment sur- [He said to us], "You will see a light [that] is more exalted than all that shines . . .

the accomplishment that accomplishes in . . . I am fully the [right hand] of the [Father who . . .] me (? or: than I) who is passes the other. And I am fully the right hand of the Father; I am in him who accomplishes." And we twelve said to him, "O Lord, in all things you have become to us salvation and life. Do you speak (or: while you speak) to us of such a hope?" And he said to us, "Have confidence and be of good courage. Truly I say to you, such a rest will be yours where there is no eating and drinking and no mourning and singing (or: care) and neither earthly garment nor perishing. And you will not have part in the creation of below, but will belong to the incorruptibility of my Father, you who will not perish. As I am continually in the Father, so also you (are) in me." And we said again to him, "In what form? Of an angel or that of flesh?" And for this he answered and said to us, "I have put on your flesh, in which I was born and died and was buried and rose again through my heavenly Father, that it might be fulfilled that was said by the prophet David concerning my death and resurrection: 'O Lord, how numerous have they become that oppress me; many have risen up against me. Many say to my soul, "He has no salvation by his God." But you, O Lord, are my refuge, my glory, and he who lifts up my head. With my voice I cried to God, and he heard me from the mount of his sanctuary. I lay down and fell asleep; and I rose

perfection." But we said [to him, "O Lord], in all [things] you have become to us [salvation and] life, proclaiming to us such a [hope]." He said to us, "Have confidence and be of a peaceful heart. Truly I say to you, your rest will be [above (?)] in the place where there is (neither) eating nor drinking, neither [rejoicing] nor mourning nor perishing of those who are [in it. You] have no part in . . . , but you will receive of the [incorruptibility of my Father. As I] am in him, so [you will be] in me."

Again [we said to him, "In what] form? In the manner of angels, or also [in flesh]?" He answered and said to us, ["Look. I have] put on [your] flesh, in which [I] was born and crucified [and] rose again through my Father who is [in heaven], that the prophecy [of the] prophet David might be fulfilled concerning what he [foretold] about me and [my] death and my resurrection, saying, 'O Lord, numerous have they become that [oppose] me, and many have risen up against me. Many say to my soul, There is no [deliverance for him] with God. [But you, O Lord, are] my protector; [you are my glory and he who lifts up] my head. With my [voice I cried out to the] Lord, and he heard me. I lay down and fell

up, for God raised me up. I was
not afraid of thousands of people
who surrounded me and rose up
against me. Arise, O Lord my
God, and save me. For you have
smitten all who show me enmity
without cause; and you have shat-
tered the teeth of sinners. Deliverance is of God, and your blessing (be) upon your people.'

asleep; I rose up, for you, O Lord,
are my protector. I will not be
afraid of tens of thousands of people who set themselves against me
round about. Rise up, O Lord;
save me, my God. For you have
cast down all who are my enemies
without cause; the teeth of sinners
you have broken. To the Lord is
salvation and his delight in his
people.'

All that was said by the prophets
was thus performed and has taken
place and is completed in me, for
I spoke in (or: by) them; how
much more will what I myself
have made known to you really
happen, that he who sent me may
be glorified by you and by those
who believe in me."

But if all the words that were
spoken by the prophets are fulfilled in me—for I was in them—
how much more will what I say to
you truly {what I say to you}
happen, that he who sent me may
be glorified by you and by those
who believe in me."

20. (Coptic: But) After he had said this to us, we said to him, "O
Lord, in all things you have shown yourself merciful to us and have
saved us; you have revealed all (Ethiopic: all this) to us. Yet (Ethiopic:
Yet one thing) might we ask you, if you permit us." (Ethiopic: And) He
answered and said to us, "I know

that you are listening and long to
listen; concerning what you wish,
ask me. Look; ask me and keep in
mind what you hear, and it will
be agreeable with me to speak
with you.

that you will carry and your heart
is pleased when you hear me. But
ask me concerning what you
wish, and I will speak well with
you.

21. (Coptic: For) Truly I say to you, as the (Coptic: my) Father
awakened me from the dead, in the same manner you also will arise

in the flesh, and he will cause you
to rise up above the heavens to
the place of which I have spoken
to you from the beginning (or:
already), which he who sent me

and be taken up above the heavens to the place of which I have
spoken to you from the beginning
(before), to the place which he
who sent me has prepared for

has prepared for you. And for this cause have I perfected all mercy: without being begotten I was born (or: begotten) of man, and without having flesh I put on flesh and grew up, that (I might regenerate) you who were begotten in the flesh, and

you. And thus will I complete all arrangements (for salvation): being unbegotten and (yet) begotten of man, being without flesh (and yet) I have worn flesh, for on that account have I come, that you . . .

(Coptic lacks about 10 lines.)

in regeneration you obtain the resurrection in your flesh, a garment that will not pass away, with all who hope and believe in him who sent me; for my Father has found pleasure in you; and to whoever I will I give the hope of the kingdom." Then we said to him, "It is great, how you cause to hope, and how you speak." He answered and said to us, "Believe (Do you believe) that everything I say to you will happen." And we answered him and said to him, "Yes, O Lord." And he said to us, "Truly I say to you that I have received all power from my Father that I may bring back those in darkness into light and those in corruptibility into incorruptibility and those in error into righteousness and those in death into life, and that those in captivity may be loosed, as what is impossible on the part of men is possible on the part of the Father. I am the hope of the hopeless, the helper of those who have no helper, the treasure of those in need, the physician of the sick, the resurrection of the dead."

22. After he had said this to us, we said to him, "O Lord, is it really in store for the flesh to be judged (together) with the soul and spirit, and will (one of these) (*Coptic:* really) rest in heaven and the other (*Coptic:* however) be punished eternally while it is (still) alive?" And (*Coptic:* But) he said to us, "How long do you still ask and inquire?"

23. And we said again to him, "O Lord,

but it is necessary, since you have commanded us to preach, prophesy, and teach, that we, having heard accurately from you, may be good preachers and may teach them, that they may believe in you. Therefore we question you."

there is a necessity upon us to inquire through you, for you command us to preach, that we ourselves may learn with certainty through you and be profitable preachers, and (that) those who will be instructed by us may believe in you. Therefore we question you frequently."

24. He answered and said to us, "Truly I say to you, the flesh

He answered us, saying, "Truly I say to you, the resurrection of the of every man will rise with his soul {alive} and his spirit."

And we said to him, "O Lord,

then can what is departed and scattered become alive? Not as if we deny it do we ask; rather we believe that what you say has happened and will happen." And he said to us, being angry, "You of little faith, how long yet do you ask me? And inquire (only) without anguish after what you wish to hear. Keep

flesh will happen while the soul and the spirit are in it."

is it then possible that what is dissolved and destroyed should be whole? Not as unbelieving do we ask you—{nor is it impossible for you}—rather we really believe that what you say will happen." And [he] was angry with us, saying to us, "O you of little faith, until what day do you ask? But what you wish, say to me, and I will tell it to you without grudging. Only keep

my commandments, and do what I tell you,

without delay and without reserve and without respect of persons; serve in the strait, direct, and narrow way. And thereby will the Father in every respect rejoice concerning you."

and do not turn away your face from anyone, that I also may not turn my face away from you; rather without delay and without reserve . . . (and) without respect of persons serve in the way that is direct and strait and oppressed (narrow). So it is also with my Father. He will rejoice concerning you."

25. And we said again to him, "O Lord, look; we have you to derision with the many questions." And he said to us,

Again [we] said to him, "O Lord, already we are ashamed that we repeatedly question and trouble [you]." Then [he] answered and said to us,

"I know that in faith and with (*Coptic:* from) your whole heart you question me. Therefore (*Ethiopic:* And) I am glad because of you. (*Coptic:* For) Truly I say to you,

I am pleased, and my Father in me rejoices, that you thus inquire and ask. Your boldness makes me rejoice, and it affords yourselves

I am [glad], and my Father who is in me, that [you] question me. For your boldness [affords me] rejoicing and gives yourselves life." And when he had said this to us, we were glad, for he had spoken to us in gentleness. And we said again to him, "Our Lord, in all things you have shown yourself gracious toward us and grant us life; for all we have asked you you have told us." Then he said to us, "Does the flesh or the spirit fall away?" And we said to him, "The flesh." And he said to us, "Now what has fallen will arise, and what is ill will be sound, that my Father may be praised therein; as he has done to me, so I (will do) to you and to all who believe in me.

[life]." But when he had said this to us we were [glad that] we asked him. And we said to him, ["O Lord, in] all things you make us alive and pity [us. Only] now will you make known to us what we will ask [you]?" Then he said to us, ["What is it] then [that pa]sses away? Is it [the flesh] or the spirit?" We said to him, "The flesh is perishable." [Then] he said to us, "What has fallen will [arise], and what is lost will be found and what is [weak] will recover, that in what is thus done [may be revealed] the glory of my Father. As [he] has done to me, so will I do to all [of you] who believe.

26. (*Coptic:* But) Truly I say to you, the flesh will rise alive with the soul, that

they may confess and be judged with the work

their accounting may take place [on] that [day], concerning what

they have done, whether it is good or bad, in order that

it may become a selection and exhibition for those who have believed and have done the commandment of my Father who sent me. Then will the righteous judgment take place; for thus my Father wills, and he said to me, 'My son, on the day of judgment you will not fear the rich and not spare the poor; rather deliver each one to eternal punishment according to his sins.' But to those who have loved me and do love me and who have done my commandment I will grant rest in life in the kingdom of my heavenly

[a] selection may take place of believers who have done the [commandments of my] Father who sent me. And thus will the judgment take place in severity. For my Father said to me, 'My son, on the day of judgment [you will neither fear] the rich nor will you [have pity on] the poor; rather according to the sin of each one will you [de]liver him to eternal punishment.' But [to my] beloved ones who have done the commandments [of my Fa]ther who sent me I will grant rest of life in the kingdom of my [Father who is

Father. Look, see what kind of power he has granted me, and he has given me, that . . . what I want and as I have wanted . . . and in whom I have awakened hope.

27. And on that account I have descended and have spoken with Abraham and Isaac and Jacob, to your fathers the prophets, and have brought to them news that they may come from the rest which is below into heaven, and have given them the right hand of the baptism of life and forgiveness and pardon for all wickedness as to you, so from now on also to those who believe in me. But whoever believes in me and does not do my commandment receives, although he believes in my name, no benefit from it. He has run a course in vain. His end is determined for ruin and for punishment of great pain, for he has sinned against my commandment.

28. But to you I have given that you should be children of the light in God and should be pure from all wickedness and from all power of the judgment (or: <archons>); and to those who believe in me through you I will do the same, and as I have said and promised to you, that he should go out of prison and should be rescued from the chains and the spears (or: <archons>) and the terrible fire." And we said to him, "O Lord, in every respect you

in] heaven, and they will see what he has granted me; and he has given me power [that I may] do what I wish, and that I may give to . . . and to those whom I have determined to give and to grant. On that account I have descended to [the place of] Lazarus, and have preached [to the righteous and] to the prophets, that they may come forth from the rest which is below and go up to what is [above] . . . right [hand] to them . . . of life and forgiveness and deliverance [from] all [evil], as I have done to you and [to those who] believe in me. But if someone believes [in me and] does not do my commandments, although he has acknowledged my name he receives no benefit from it and has [run a] futile course. For such will be in error and in [ruin, since they have] disregarded my commandments.

[But so much more you], the children of life, I have redeemed from all evil and from [the power of the] archons, and all who through you will believe [in] me. For what I have promised [you I] will also give to them, that they may come [out of] the prison and the chains of the archons and the powerful fire." We answered and said to him, "O Lord, you have given rest of [. . us] and have given . . . in wonders to . . . of faith; will you yourself now have made us rejoice and have given us rest; for in faithfulness and truthfulness you have preached to our fathers and to the prophets, and even so to us and to every man." And he said to us, "Truly I say to you, you and all who believe and also they who yet will believe in him who sent me I will cause to rise up into heaven, to the place which the Father has prepared for the elect and most elect, (the Father) who will give the rest that he has promised, and eternal life.

29. But those who have sinned against my commandment, who teach something else, subtract from and add to and work for their own glory, alienating those who rightly believe in me. . . ." And we said to him, "O Lord, will there exist another teaching and grievance (?)?" And he said to us, "As those who fulfil what is good and beautiful, so (also) the wicked shall be manifest. And then a righteous judgment will take place according to their work, how they have acted; and they will be delivered to ruin." And we said to him, "Blessed are we, for we see and hear you as you speak to us, and our eyes have seen such mighty deeds that you have done." And he answered and said to us, "But much more blessed will they be who do not see me and (yet) believe in me, for they will be called children of the kingdom and (will be)

preach these things . . . , after you have preached to the fathers and to the prophets?" Then he said to [us], "Truly I say to you, [all] who have believed in me [and who will] believe in him who sent me I will [lead] up to heaven, to the place [which] my Father has [prepared] for the elect, and I will give you the chosen kingdom in rest, and eternal life.

But those who have transgressed [my] commandments and have taught another teaching, while they . . . what is written and add to . . . own . . . teaching with other words [those who] believe in me rightly, if [they] are brought to ruin by such '. . . eternal punishment." [But] we said [to him], "O Lord, then [will] there exist teaching from [others], besides what [you] have told us?" [. . .] us, "It is necessary that they exist, that [what is] evil and what is good should be manifest. And thus will the judgment of those who do these works be revealed, and [according to their] works will they be judged and delivered to death." [We] said again to him, "O Lord, blessed are we, [. . .] you and hear you as you [preach] such things, for our eyes have seen these great wonders that you have done." He [answered and said] to us, "Much more blessed

perfect in the perfect one; to these I will become eternal life in the kingdom of my Father." And we said again to him, "O Lord, how will it be possible to believe that you will leave us, as you said: there is coming a time and an hour when it is in store for you to go to your Father?"

30. He answered and said to us, "Go and preach to the twelve tribes of Israel and to the Gentiles and Israel and to the land of Israel towards East and West, North and South; and many will believe in me, the son of God." And we said to him, "O Lord, who will believe us and who will listen to us and how can we do and teach and tell the wonders and signs and mighty deeds, as you have done?" And he answered and said to us, "Go and preach {and teach} concerning {the coming and} the mercy of my Father. As my Father has done through me, I will also do through you in that I am with you, and I will give you my peace and my spirit and my power, {that it may happen to you} that they believe. Also to them will this power be given and transmitted that they may give it to the Gentiles.

are they who have not seen and (yet) have believed, for such will be called [children] of the kingdom, [and they] will be perfect [in] the perfect one [and] I will be life [to them] in the kingdom of my Father." Again [we said to him], "O Lord, in what way will one be able to believe [that you] will go and leave us, as you [said] to us, 'A day will come [and an hour] when I shall go up to my Father'?" But [he] said to [us], "Go you and preach to the twelve tribes and preach also to the Gentiles and to the whole land of Israel from [sunrise] to sunset and from [South to] North, and many will believe [in the] son of God." But we said to him, "[O Lord], who will believe us or [who] will listen to us while we do, teach, and tell the powers and the signs that [you] have done, and the [wonders]?" Then he answered and said to us, "[Go] and preach the mercy [of my] Father; and what he has done through me [will I my] self do through you in that I am in you, [and] I will give you my peace, and from my spirit I will give you a power that you may prophesy to them to eternal life. But to the others will I myself also give my power, that they may teach the other nations.
(*Coptic lacks 6 leaves.*)

31. And look; you will meet a man whose name is Saul, which being interpreted means Paul. He is a Jew, circumcised according to the command of the law; and he will hear my voice from heaven with terror, fear, and trembling; and his eyes will be darkened and by your hand be crossed with spittle. And do all to him as I have done to you. Deliver (?) (him?) to others. And this man—immediately his eyes will be opened, and he will praise God, my heavenly Father. And he will become strong among the nations and will preach and teach, and many will be delighted when they hear and will be saved. Then will he be hated and delivered into the hand of his enemy, and he will testify before mortal kings, and upon him will come the completion of the testimony to me; because he had persecuted and hated me, he will be converted to me and preach and teach, and he will be among my elect, a chosen vessel and a wall that does not fall. The last of the last will become a preacher to the Gentiles, perfect in (or: through) the will of my Father. As you have learned from the Scriptures that your fathers the prophets spoke concerning me, and it is fulfilled in me"—this certain thing he said—"so you must become a leader to them. And every word which I have spoken to you and which you have written concerning me, that I am the word of the Father and the Father is in me, so you must become also to that man, as it befits you. Teach and remind (him) what has been said in the Scriptures and fulfilled concerning me, and then he will be for the salvation of the Gentiles."

32. And we said to him, "O master, do we have together with them one hope of the inheritance?" He answered and said to us, "Are the fingers of the hand alike or the ears of corn in the field? Or do the fruit-bearing trees give the same fruit? Do they not bring forth fruit according to their nature?" And we said to him, "O Lord, are you speaking again in parables to us?" And he said to us, "Do not be grieved. Truly I say to you, you are my brothers, companions in the kingdom of heaven with my Father, for so has it pleased him. Truly I say to you, also to those whom you shall have taught and who have become believers in me will I give this hope."

33. And we said again to him, "When, Lord, will we meet that man, and when will you go to your Father and to our God and Lord?" And he answered and said to us, "That man will set out from the land of Cilicia to Damascus in Syria to tear asunder the Church which you must create. It is I who will speak (to him) through you, and he will come quickly. He will be strong in his faith, that the word of the prophet may be fulfilled where it says, 'Behold, out of the land of Syria I will begin to call a new Jerusalem, and I will subdue Zion and it will be captured; and the barren one who has no children will be fruitful and will be called the daughter of my Father, but to me, my bride; for so has it pleased him who sent me.' But that man will I turn aside, that

he may not go there and complete his evil plan. And glory of my Father will come in through him. For after I have gone away and remain with my Father, I will speak with him from heaven; and it will all happen as I have predicted to you concerning him."

34. And we said again to him, "O Lord, such meaningful things you have spoken and preached to us and have revealed to us great things never yet spoken, and in every respect you have comforted us and have shown yourself gracious to us. For after your resurrection you revealed all this to us that we might be really saved. But you told us only that signs and wonders would happen in heaven and upon earth before the end of the world comes. Teach us, that we thus may recognize it." And he said to us, "I will teach you, and not only what will happen to you, but (also) to those whom you shall teach and who shall believe; and there are such as will hear {this man(?)} and will believe in me. In those years and in those days this will happen." And we said to him again, "O Lord, what is it then that will happen?" And he said to us, "Then will the believers and also they who do not believe see a trumpet in heaven, and the sight of great stars that are visible while it is day, and a dragon reaching from heaven to earth, and stars that are like fire falling down and great hailstones of severe (?) fire; and how sun and moon fight against each other, and constantly the frightening of thunder and lightning, thunderclaps and earthquakes, how cities fall down and in their ruin men die, constant drought from the failing of the rain, a great plague and an extensive and often quick death, so that those who die will lack a grave; and the going out (or: carrying out) of children and relatives will be on one bed (or: bier). And the relative will not turn toward his child, nor the child to his relative; and a man will not turn toward his neighbour. But those forsaken who were left behind will rise up and see those who forsook them when they brought them out because (there was) plague. Everything is hatred and affliction and jealousy, and they will take from the one and give to another; and what comes after this will be worse than this.

35. Then my Father will become angry because of the wickedness of men; for their offences are many and the horror of their impurity is much against them in the corruption of their life." And we said to him, "What, Lord, what (is allotted) to those who hope in you?" And he answered and said to us, "How long are you still slow of heart? Truly I say to you, as the prophet David has spoken concerning me and my people, so will it also be concerning those who shall believe in me. But there will be in the world deceivers and enemies of

righteousness, and they will meet the prophecy of David who said, 'Their feet are quick to shed blood and their tongue weaves deceit, and the venom of serpents is under their lips. And I see you as you wander with a thief and your share is with a fornicator. While you sit there furthermore you slander your brother, and set a trap for the son of your mother. What do you think? Should I be like you?' And now see how the prophet of God has spoken concerning everything, that all may be fulfilled that was said before."

36. And we said to him again, "O Lord, will the Gentiles then not say, 'Where is their God?' " He answered and said to us, "Thus will the elect be revealed, in that they go out after they have been afflicted by such a distress." And we said to him, "Will their exit from the world (take place) through a plague that has tormented them?" And he said to us, "No, but if they suffer torment, such suffering will be a test for them, whether they have faith and whether they keep in mind these words of mine and obey my commandment. They will rise up, and their waiting will last (only a) few days, that he who sent me may be glorified, and I with him. For he has sent me to you. I tell you this. But you tell (it) to Israel and to the Gentiles, that they may hear; they also are to be saved and believe in me and escape the distress of the plague. And whoever has escaped the distress of death, such a one will be taken and kept in prison, under torture like that of a thief." And we said to him, "O Lord, will they be like unto the unbelievers, and will you likewise punish those who have escaped the plague?" And he said to us, "Believing in my name they have done the work of sinners; they have acted like unbelievers." And we said again to him, "O Lord, have they who have escaped in this part no life?" He answered and said to us, "Whoever has done the glorification of my Father, he is the dwelling-place of my Father."

37. And we said to him, "O Lord, teach us what will happen after this." And he said to us, "In those years and days there shall be war upon war, and the four corners of the world will be shaken and will make war upon each other. And then a disturbance of the clouds (will take place), darkness and drought and persecution of those who believe in me, and of the elect. Then dissension, conflict, and evil of action against each other. Among them there are some who believe in my name and (yet) follow evil and teach vain teaching. And men will follow them and will submit themselves to their riches, their depravity, their mania for drinking, and their gifts of bribery; and respect of persons will rule among them.

38. But those who desire to see the face of God and who do not

regard the person of the sinful rich and who do not fear the men who lead them astray, but reprove them, they will be <crowned> in the presence of the Father, as also those who reprove their neighbours will be saved. This is a son of wisdom and of faith. But if he does not become a son of wisdom, then he will hate and persecute and not turn towards

his brother, and will despise (him) and cast him away.

his neighbour, will turn against him and . . . him.

But those who walk in truth and in the knowledge of faith

in me and have the knowledge of wisdom and perseverance for righteousness' sake, in that men despise those who strive for poverty and they (nevertheless) endure—great is their reward. Those who are reviled, tormented, persecuted, since they are destitute and men are arrogant against them and they hunger and thirst and because they have persevered—blessed will they be in heaven, and they will be there with me always. Woe to those who hate and despise them! And their end is for destruction."

possessing love for me—for they have endured abuse—they will be proud, walking in poverty and tolerating those who hate them [and] revile them. They have been [tormented], being destitute, since men were arrogant against them while they walk in hunger and thirst; but because they have persevered . . . the blessedness of heaven, they also will be with me eternally. But woe to those who walk in pride and boasting, for their end is destruction."

39. And we said to him, "O Lord, will all this happen?" And he said to us, "How will the judgment of righteousness take place for the sinners and the righteous?" And we said to him, "Will they not in that day say to you, 'You caused to lead toward righteousness and sin and have separated darkness and light, evil and good'?" And he said to us, "Adam was given the power that he might choose what he wanted from the two; and he chose the light and stretched out his hand

But we said to him, "O Lord, what is yours is this, that you do not let us come upon them." But he answered and said to us, "How will the judgment come about? Either of the righteous or of the unrighteous?" But we said to him, "O Lord, in that day they will say to you, 'You did not pursue [righteousness] and unrighteousness, light and darkness, evil and good.' " Then he said, "I will answer them saying, 'Adam was given the power to choose one of [the] two. He chose the and took (it) and left the darkness and withdrew from it (or: <put it away from himself>). Likewise every man is given the ability to believe in the light; this is the life of the Father who sent me. And whoever has believed in me will live, if he has done the work of light. But if he acknowledges that it is light and does what is (characteristic) of darkness, then he has neither anything that he can say in defence nor will he be able to raise his face and look at the son, which (Son) I am. And I will say to him, 'You have sought and found, have asked and received. What do you blame us for? Why did you withdraw from me and my kingdom? You have acknowledged me and (yet) denied.' Now therefore see that each one is able to live as well as to die. And whoever does my commandment and keeps it will be a son of the light, i.e. of my Father. And for those who keep and do (it), for their sake I came down from heaven; I, the word, became flesh and died, teaching and guiding, that some shall be saved, but the others eternally ruined, being punished by fire in flesh and spirit."

40. And we said to him, "O Lord, we are truly troubled on their account." And he said to us, "You do well, for so are the righteous anxious about the sinners,

light and put his hand upon it; but he forsook the darkness and cast it from him. So have all men the power to believe in the light which is [life] and which is the Father who sent me.' But everyone who believes (and) does the works of light will live in them. But if there is someone who acknowledges that he is reckoned to the light, while he does the works of darkness—such a one has no defence to make, nor will he be able to lift up his face to [look at the] son of God, which (Son) I am. I will say to him, 'As you sought you have found, and as you asked you have received. In what do you condemn me, O man? Why did you leave me and deny me? Why did you acknowledge me and (yet) deny me? Does not every man have the power to live or to die?' Now whoever has kept my commandments will be a son of light, i.e. of the Father who is in me. But on account of those who pervert my words I have come down from heaven. I am the Logos; I became flesh, labouring and teaching that those who are called will be saved, and the lost will be lost eternally. They will be [tormented] alive and will be scourged in [their] flesh and in their soul."

But we said to him, "O Lord, truly we are anxious on their account." But he said to us, "You do well, for the righteous are anxious about the sinners, and

and they pray and implore God and ask him." And we said to him, "O Lord, does no one entreat you?" And he said to us, "Yes, I will hear the requests of the righteous concerning them." And we said to him, "O Lord, all this you have taught us, and have stimulated us and have proved gracious toward us. And we will preach it to those to whom it is fitting. But will there be for us a reward with you?"

41. And he said to us, "Go and preach and be good ministers and servants." And we said to him, "O Lord, you are our father." And he said to us, "Are all fathers and all servants, all teachers?" And we said to him, "O Lord, did you not say, 'Do not call (anyone) on earth father and master, for one is your father and teacher, he who is in heaven'? Now you say to us that we should like you become fathers to many children and also teachers and servants." And he answered and said to us, "You have rightly said. Truly I say to you, all who have listened to you and have believed in me will receive the light of the seal that is in my hand, and through me you will become fathers and teachers."

42. And we said to him, "O Lord, how is it possible for these three to be in one?" And he answered and said to us, "Truly, truly I say to you, you will be

pray for them, asking my Father." Again we said to him, "O Lord, now why is no one afraid of you?" But he said to us, "Yes, I will hear the prayer of the righteous that they make for them." But when he had said this to us, we said to him, "O Lord, in all things you have taught us {. . .} and pitied us and saved us, that we may preach to those who are worthy to be saved, and that we may earn a reward with you."

[But] he answered and said to us, "Go, and preach; thus you will become workers . . . and servants." But we said to him, "You it is who will preach through us." Then he answered us saying, "Do not be all fathers nor all masters." We said to him, "O Lord, it is you who said, 'Do not call (anyone) father upon earth, for one is your father who is in heaven and your master.' Why do you now say to us, 'You will be fathers of many children and servants and masters'?" But he answered and said to us, "As you have said. For truly I say to you, whoever will hear you and believe in me, he [will receive from] you the light of the seal through [me] and baptism through me; you will [become] fathers and servants and also masters."

But we said to him, "O Lord, how now (is it possible) that each one of us should become these three?" But he said to us, "Truly I say to you, you will first of all be called

called fathers, for you, full of love and compassion, have revealed to them what (is) in heaven (. . . for) by my hand they will receive the baptism of life and forgiveness of sin. And teachers, for you have delivered to them my word without anguish and have warned them and they have turned back in the things for which you rebuked them. And you were not afraid of their riches and did not respect the face (or: the person), but you kept the commandment of the Father and did it. And you have a reward with my heavenly Father; and they shall have forgiveness of sins and eternal life and a share of the kingdom." And we said to him, "O Lord, if they had a ten-thousandfold mouth, they would not be able to give thanks to you as it is fitting." And he answered and said to us, "I say this to you that you may do as I have done to you;

43. and be as the wise virgins who kindled the light and did not slumber and who went with their lamps to meet the lord, the bridegroom, and have gone in with him into the bridegroom's chamber. But the foolish ones who talked with them were not able to watch, but fell asleep." And we said to him, "O Lord, who are the wise and who the foolish?" And he said to us, "The wise are these

fathers, for you have revealed to them with seemly hearts and in love the things of the kingdom of heaven. And you will be called servants, for they will receive by my hand through you the baptism of life and the forgiveness of their sins. And you will be called masters, for you have given them the word without grudging and have warned them; and when you warned them they turned back. You were not afraid of their riches [and of] their face, but you kept [the commandments] of my Father and performed them. And you will have [a] great reward with my Father who is in heaven, and they shall have forgiveness of sins and eternal life, and will have a part in the kingdom of heaven." But we said to him, "O Lord, even if each one of us had ten thousand tongues to speak with, we would not be able to give thanks to you, for you promise us such things." Then he answered, saying, "Only do what I say to you, as I myself have also done; and you will be like the wise virgins who watched and did not sleep, but [went] out to the lord into the bridechamber. But [the foolish] were not able to watch, but fell asleep." But we said to him, "O Lord, who are the wise and who are the foolish?" He said to us, "Five wise and five foolish, these with respect to whom the prophet said, 'They are children of God.' Now hear their names."

five, who are called by the prophet daughters of God, whose names let men hear." But we were sad and troubled and wept for those who had been shut out. And he said to us, "The five wise are these: Faith, Love, Joy, Peace, Hope. As soon as they who believe in me have these, they will be leaders to those who believe in me and in him who sent me. I am the Lord and I am the bridegroom; they have received me and have gone with me into the house of the bridegroom, and laid themselves down (at table) with the bridegroom and rejoiced. But the five foolish slept, and when they awoke they came to the house of the bridegroom and knocked at the doors, for they had been shut; and they wept, because they were shut." And we said to him, "O Lord, now these their wise sisters who (are) in the house—do they not open to them and are they not sorrowful on their account?" And he said to us, "Yes, they are sorrowful and concerned on their account and entreat the bridegroom and are not yet able to obtain (anything) on their account." And we said to him, "O Lord, when will they go in for their sisters' sakes?" And he said to us, "Whoever is shut out is shut out." And we said to him, "O Lord, is this thing definite? Who now are these foolish ones?" And he said to us, "Listen: Insight, Knowledge, Obedience,

But we wept and were sad about those who had fallen asleep. He said to us, "The five wise are Faith and Love and Grace, Peace, and Hope. Among those who believe they who have these will be guides to those who have believed in me and in him who sent me. I am the Lord and I am the bridegroom whom they have received, and they have gone into the house of the [bridegroom] and have laid themselves down with me in my [bride]chamber [and rejoiced]. But the five foolish, when [they] had fallen asleep (?), they awoke, came to the door of the bridechamber and knocked, for they had been shut out. Then they wept and grieved that it was not opened for them." But we said to him, "O Lord, and their wise sisters who were within in the house of the bridegroom, did they remain in there without opening to them, and did they not grieve on their account or did they not pray the bridegroom to open to them?" He answered saying, "They were not yet able to find grace on their behalf." We said to him, "O Lord, on what day will they go in for their sisters' sakes?" [Then] he said to us, "Whoever [is shut out] is shut out." But we said to him, "O Lord, is this [. . .]? Now who are the foolish?" He said to us, "Hear their names. They are Knowledge and Insight, Obedience, Forbearance, and Mercy. These are they

got to remember this isn't Jesus speaking

Endurance, Mercy. These have slept in those who have believed and acknowledged me.

44. And since those who slept did not fulfil my commandment, they will be outside the kingdom and the fold of the shepherd; and whoever remains outside the fold will the wolf eat. And although he hears he will be judged and will die, and much suffering and distress and endurance will come upon him; and although he is badly pained and although he is cut into pieces and lacerated with long and painful punishment, yet he will not be able to die quickly."

45. And we said to him, "O Lord, you have revealed everything to us well." And he said to us, "Understand and apprehend these words." And we said to him, "O Lord, these five it is through which they have the expectation of going into your kingdom; and five who are shut out through which they will be outside your kingdom. Yet they who have watched and who have gone in with the Lord, the bridegroom, will not rejoice because of those who slept." And he said to us, "They will rejoice that they have gone in with the Lord, and will be grieved on account of those who slept; for they are their sisters. And these daughters of God are ten." And we said to him, "O Lord, it suits your greatness that you show grace to their sisters."

which slept in those who have believed and acknowledged me.

But my commandments were not fulfilled by those who slept. Consequently they will remain outside the kingdom and the fold of the [shepherd] and his sheep. But whoever remains outside [the fold] of the sheep will the wolves eat, and he will . . . , dying in much suffering. [Rest] and perseverance will not be [in] him, and he [will] be badly (?) tormented that he . . . [and they will punish] him in great [punishment, and he will] be under tortures."

[But we said to him], "O Lord, you have revealed everything [to us] well." Then he answered [say]ing to us, "Do you not apprehend these words?" We said to him, "Yes, O Lord; through the five will they come into your kingdom. Yet they who watched and were with you, the Lord and bridegroom, will nevertheless not rejoice because of those who slept." He said to us, "They [will rejoice] that they have gone in with the bridegroom, the Lord; and they are troubled on account of those who [slept], for they are their sisters. The ten are the daughters of God the Father." We [then said] to him, ["O Lord], it is yours that you . . ." He said to us, ". . . , but his who sent me, and [I] agree with him.

And he said to us, "This thing is not yours, but his who sent me, and I also agree with him.

46. But you, as you go, preach and teach truly and rightly, respecting and fearing the person of no one, but especially (not) that of the rich, among whom (something) will be found, who do not do my commandment, who revel in their riches." And we said to him, "O Lord, do you speak to us only of the rich?" And he said to us, "Also of him who is not rich; as soon as he gives and does not deny to him who has nothing, of such a one (I say this:) he will be called by men a doer.

47. But if someone should fall bearing his burden, i.e. the sin he has committed against the person of his neighbour, then his neighbour should admonish him (in return) for what (good) he has done to his neighbour. And when his neighbour has admonished him and he has returned, then he will be saved, and he who has admonished him will obtain eternal life. But if he sees how this one who renders him (service) sins, and encourages him, such a one will be judged in a great judgment. For a blind man who leads a blind man, both will fall into a ditch. Even so the one who encourages, who respects the person, and also the one whom he encourages and whose person he respects, will both be punished with one punishment, as the

But you preach and teach in uprightness (and) well, hesitating before no one and fearing no one, but especially (not) the rich, for they do not do my commandments, but revel(?) in their riches." But we said to him, "O Lord, if [it] is the rich [alone]?" He answered saying [to us, "If] anyone who is not rich and possesses [a little] property gives to the needy [and to the poor], then men will call him a bene[factor].

But if [someone] should fall [under the] load because of the sins he has [committed, then let] his neighbour admonish him for [the good that] he has done to his neighbour. Now if his neighbour [has admonished] him and he returns he will be saved; (and) he who admonished him will receive a reward and live for ever. For a needy man, if he sees someone sinning who has done him good, and does not admonish him, then he will be judged in an evil judgment. But a blind man who leads a blind man, [both] fall into [a] ditch. And whoever regards the person for [their] sake, [he will be like] the two, as the pro[phet said], 'Woe to those who regard the person and [justify the ungodly] for the sake of gifts, whose [God is] their belly.' See now that prophet said, 'Woe to those who encourage, who speak fair to the sinner for the sake of a bribe, whose God is their belly.' You see how the judgment is? Truly I say to you, in that day I will not fear the rich and will have no pity for the poor.

48. If you have seen with your eyes how (someone) sins, then correct him, you alone (or: under four eyes). If he listens to you, then you have won him. But if he does not listen to you, then come out with one or at the most two others; correct your brother. But if he (even then) does not listen to you, so shall he be to you as a Gentile and a tax collector.

a judgment [is appointed for them]. For truly I say [to you, in] that day I will neither fear [the] rich nor have sympathy with the [poor].

If you see a sinner, then [admonish him] between yourself and him. But if he does not listen to [you, then take] with you another up to three and instruct your brother. If he will not listen to you again, then set him before you as . . ."

(Here the Coptic text breaks off.)

49. If you hear something, then do not give any belief against your brother and do not slander and do not love to listen to slander. For it is written, 'Let your ear listen to nothing against your brother, but (only) if you have seen, censure, correct, and convert him.' " And we said to him, "Lord, you have taught and exhorted us in everything. But, Lord, among the believers who among them believe in the preaching of your name should there be dissension and dispute and envy and confusion and hatred and distress? For you have nevertheless said, 'They will find fault with one another and have not regarded the person (or: without regarding the person).' Do these sin who hate the one who has corrected them?" And he answered and said to us, "Now why will the judgment take place? That the wheat may be put in its barn and its chaff thrown into the fire.

50. . . . Who thus hate, and he who loves me and finds fault with those who do not do my commandments, these will thus be hated and persecuted, and men will despise and mock (them). They will also deliberately say what is not (true), and there will come a conspiracy against those who love me. But these will rebuke them that they may be saved. And those who will find fault with them and correct and exhort them will be hated and set apart and despised; and those who wish (to) do good to them will be prevented (from it). But those who

have endured this will be as martyrs with the Father, for they were zealous concerning righteousness and were not zealous with corruptible zeal." And we said to him, "Will such, Lord, also happen in our midst?" And he said to us, "Do not fear what will happen not with many, but (only) with few." And we said to him, "Tell us in what way." And he said to us, "There will come another teaching and a conflict; and in that they seek their own glory and produce worthless teaching an offence of death will come thereby, and they will teach and turn away from my commandment even those who believe in me and bring them out of eternal life. But woe to those who use my word and my commandment for a pretext, and also to those who listen to them and to those who turn away from the life of the teaching, {to those who turn away from the commandment of life,} they will be eternally punished with them."

51. And after he had said this and had ended the discourse with us, he said again to us, "Look. After three days and three hours he who sent me will come that I may go with him." And as he spoke there was thunder and lightning and an earthquake, and the heavens divided and a bright cloud came and took him away. And we heard the voice of many angels as they rejoiced and praised and said, "Assemble us, O priest, in the light of glory." And when he had come near to the firmament of heaven, we heard him say, "Go in peace."

goofy

The Acts of Pilate

The Acts of Pilate (Acts Pilate) *is a document of Christian apologetics that endeavors to introduce its readers to some of the beliefs of a Christian community and to defend the claim of its members to be the true citizens of the people of God. This is attempted by giving a somewhat elaborate account of Jesus' trial before Pilate, his crucifixion and burial, reports of the empty tomb, and an alleged discussion of his resurrection by a council of the leaders of the Jews. This document was incorporated into the* Gospel of Nicodemus, *with which it was transmitted in the Middle Ages. The prologue of the* Acts of Pilate *states that it was written in Hebrew by Nicodemus shortly after Jesus' death, and translated into Greek ca. 425 C.E. by one Ananias. In fact, this prologue is almost certainly a secondary addition to a more original work, which undoubtedly was written in Greek.*

There were several documents pertaining to the alleged activities of Pilate, the Roman procurator who had Jesus killed, in circulation in the early church. Justin (a church apologist who lived in the middle of the second century) twice referred to a document entitled the Acts of Pontius Pilate. *His matter-of-fact introduction to this document, using a quotation formula closely related to those formulas he employed in his citations of the gospel "Memoirs" of Matthew and Luke and of the writings of the Jewish scriptures, makes it likely that he was referring to an actual document known to him and transmitted under Pilate's name. Early in the fourth century, Eusebius made mention of "forged" Reports of Pilate, written to repudiate the Christian faith. It is likely that such reports were written in response to previous Christian claims that Pilate became a witness to the death and resurrection of Jesus. Late in the fourth century, Epiphanius appears to refer to the document that we now possess, for when he states that a group of Christians thought they could accurately determine the date of Jesus' passion by using a work entitled the* Acts of Pilate, *the date he gives is identical with that recorded in the prologue to the work we have. The original Greek is extant in several medieval manuscripts, of which the earliest dates from the twelfth century; these manuscripts have been arranged stemmatically into two recensions, of which the longer recension seems to preserve the better text. The translation of the* Acts of Pilate *into numerous ancient languages is indicative of its influence in the church throughout the centuries.*

The written sources of the Acts of Pilate *are the Jewish scriptures and the Gospels of Matthew, Mark, Luke, and John. The Jewish scriptures are cited as proof texts in order to confirm that interpretation which viewed Jesus as the fulfillment of Jewish expectations and his fate as the culmination of the events of their history. In accordance with this view, the followers of Jesus are understood to be the legitimate heirs of the Jewish traditions, the embodiment of the allegedly "chosen" people of God.*

The gospels of the New Testament are cited as "historical" texts that record the dramatic, final events of Jesus' life. No longer is it a question of primitive creeds or catechisms, sayings or stories which structure a text, but of written gospels of a church. Thus, the attempt to understand the death of Jesus, that apologetic impulse which ignited the initial reflections of the earliest believers in Jesus, has been converted into the understanding of the will of God at work in the activities of Jesus and his followers. The exoneration of Pilate and the accompanying anti-Jewish polemic are consonant with this interpretation. Pilate is now portrayed as a witness for the historicity of the death and resurrection of Jesus, and hence, for the truth of Christianity. The Gospel of Matthew's interpretation of the destruction of the Temple in Jerusalem as a consequence of the death of Jesus (Matt. 27:24–25), moreover, is made even more explicit in the Acts of Pilate. *And even Jesus himself is made to state that Moses and the prophets foretold his death and resurrection.*

The Acts of Pilate *was composed sometime after the four gospels of the New Testament and before the first certain attestation of the text in the writings of Epiphanius. If Justin referred to a work such as this, then the earliest possible date of composition would be sometime in the mid- to late second century. The latest likely date would be in the third century, when all four gospels of the New Testament came to be employed collectively in the service of Christian apologetics. Identifying the provenance of the* Acts of Pilate *is difficult. Syria is perhaps most plausible, but a location in Asia Minor, Rome, or Egypt is not impossible.*

The text is numbered, following the prologue, according to chapter and verse divisions (1.1–16.8). The translation was made by Felix Scheidweiler and A. J. B. Higgins (New Testament Apocrypha).

The Acts of Pilate

I, Ananias, an officer of the guard, being learned in the law, came to know our Lord Jesus Christ from the sacred scriptures, which I approached with faith, and was accounted worthy of holy baptism. And having searched for the reports made at that period in the time of our Lord Jesus Christ <and for that> which the Jews committed to writing under Pontius Pilate, I found these acts in the Hebrew language and according to God's good pleasure I translated them into Greek for the information of all those who call upon the name of our Lord Jesus Christ, in the eighteenth year of the reign of our Emperor Flavius Theodosius and in the fifth year of the "Nobility" of Flavius Valentinianus, in the ninth indiction.

Therefore all you who read this and copy it out, remember me and pray for me that God may be gracious to me and forgive my sins which I have sinned against him. Peace be to those who read and hear it, and to their servants. Amen.

In the nineteenth year of the reign of the Roman Emperor Tiberius, when Herod was king of Galilee, in the nineteenth year of his rule, on the eighth day before the Kalends of April, that is, the 25th of March, in the consulate of Rufus and Rubellio, in the fourth year of the two hundred and second Olympiad, when Joseph Caiaphas was high priest of the Jews.

What Nicodemus after the passion of the Lord upon the cross recorded and delivered concerning the conduct of the chief priests and the rest of the Jews—and the same Nicodemus drew up his records in the Hebrew language—runs approximately as follows:

1. 1. The chief priests and scribes assembled in council, Annas and Caiaphas, Semes, Dathaes and Gamaliel, Judas, Levi and Nephthalim, Alexander and Jairus and the rest of the Jews, and came to Pilate

accusing Jesus of many deeds. They said: "We know that this man is the son of Joseph the carpenter and was born of Mary; but he says he is the Son of God and a king. Moreover he pollutes the Sabbath and wishes to destroy the law of our fathers." Pilate said: "And what things does he do that he wishes to destroy it?" The Jews say: "We have a law that we should not heal anyone on the Sabbath. But this man with his evil deeds has healed on the Sabbath the lame, the bent, the withered, the blind, the paralytic, and the possessed." Pilate asked them: "With what evil deeds?" They answered him: "He is a sorcerer, and by Beelzebub the prince of the devils he casts out evil spirits, and all are subject to him." Pilate said to them: "This is not to cast out demons by an unclean spirit, but by the god Asclepius."

2. The Jews said to Pilate: "We beseech your excellency to place him before your judgment-seat and to try him." And Pilate called them to him and said: "Tell me! How can I, a governor, examine a king?" They answered: "We do not say that he is a king, but he says he is." And Pilate summoned his messenger and said to him: "Let Jesus be brought with gentleness." So the messenger went out, and when he perceived him, he did him reverence, and taking the kerchief which was in his hand, he spread it upon the ground, and said to him: "Lord, walk on this and go in, for the governor calls you." But when the Jews saw what the messenger had done, they cried out against Pilate and said: "Why did you not order him to come in by a herald, but by a messenger? For as soon as he saw him the messenger reverenced him, and spread out his kerchief on the ground, and made him walk on it like a king."

3. Then Pilate called for the messenger and said to him: "Why have you done this, and spread your kerchief on the ground and made Jesus walk on it?" The messenger answered him: "Lord governor, when you sent me to Jerusalem to Alexander, I saw him sitting on an ass, and the children of the Hebrews held branches in their hands and cried out; and others spread their garments before him, saying: 'Save now, thou that art in the highest! Blessed is he that comes in the name of the Lord!' "

4. The Jews cried out to the messenger: "The children of the Hebrews cried out in Hebrew; how do you know it in Greek?" The messenger replied: "I asked one of the Jews, and said: What is it that they cry out in Hebrew? And he interpreted it to me." Pilate said to them: "And what did they cry out in Hebrew?" The Jews answered: "Hosanna membrome baruchamma adonai." Pilate asked again: "And the Hosanna and the rest, how is it translated?" The Jews replied:

"Save now, thou that art in the highest. Blessed is he that comes in the name of the Lord." Pilate said to them: "If you testify to the words of the children, what sin has the messenger committed?" And they were silent. The governor said to the messenger: "Go out and bring him in in whatever you wish." And the messenger went out and did as before and said to Jesus: "Enter, the governor calls you."

5. Now when Jesus entered in, and the standard-bearers were holding the standards, the images of the emperor on the standards bowed and did reverence to Jesus. And when the Jews saw the behaviour of the standards, how they bowed down and did reverence to Jesus, they cried out loudly against the standard-bearers. But Pilate said to them: "Do you not marvel how the images bowed and did reverence to Jesus?" The Jews said to Pilate: "We saw how the standard-bearers lowered them and reverenced him." And the governor summoned the standard-bearers and asked them: "Why did you do this?" They answered: "We are Greeks and servers of temples, and how could we reverence him? We held the images; but they bowed down of their own accord and reverenced him."

6. Then Pilate said to the rulers of the synagogue and the elders of the people: "Choose strong men to carry the standards, and let us see whether the images bow by themselves." So the elders of the Jews took twelve strong men and made them carry the standards by sixes, and they were placed before the judgment-seat of the governor. And Pilate said to the messenger: "Take him out of the praetorium and bring him in again in whatever way you wish." And Jesus left the praetorium with the messenger. And Pilate summoned those who before carried the images, and said to them: "I have sworn by the safety of Caesar that, if the standards do not bow down when Jesus enters, I will cut off your heads." And the governor commanded Jesus to enter in the second time. And the messenger did as before and besought Jesus to walk upon his kerchief. He walked upon it and entered in. And when he had entered in, the standards bowed down again and did reverence to Jesus.

2. 1. When Pilate saw this he was afraid, and sought to rise from the judgment-seat. And while he was still thinking of rising up, his wife sent to him saying: Have nothing to do with this righteous man. For I have suffered many things because of him by night. And Pilate summoned all the Jews, and stood up and said to them: "You know that my wife fears God and favours rather the customs of the Jews, with you." They answered him: "Yes, we know it." Pilate said to them: "See, my wife sent to me saying: Have nothing to do with this

righteous man. For I have suffered many things because of him by night." The Jews answered Pilate: "Did we not tell you that he is a sorcerer? Behold, he has sent a dream to your wife." 2. And Pilate called Jesus to him and said to him: "What do these men testify against you? Do you say nothing?" Jesus answered: "If they had no power, they would say nothing; for each man has power over his own mouth, to speak good and evil. They shall see (to it)."

3. Then the elders of the Jews answered and said to Jesus: "What should we see? Firstly, that you were born of fornication; secondly, that your birth meant the death of the children in Bethlehem; thirdly, that your father Joseph and your mother Mary fled into Egypt because they counted for nothing among the people." 4. Then declared some of the Jews that stood by, devout men: "We deny that he came of fornication, for we know that Joseph was betrothed to Mary, and he was not born of fornication." Pilate then said to the Jews who said that he came of fornication: "Your statement is not true; for there was a betrothal, as your own fellow-countrymen say." Annas and Caiaphas say to Pilate: "We, the whole multitude, cry out that he was born of fornication, and we are not believed; these are proselytes and disciples of his." And Pilate called to him Annas and Caiaphas and said to them: "What are proselytes?" They answered: "They were born children of Greeks, and now have become Jews." Then said those who said that he was not born of fornication, namely Lazarus, Asterius, Antonius, Jacob, Amnes, Zeras, Samuel, Isaac, Phineës, Crispus, Agrippa, and Judas: "We are not proselytes, but are children of Jews and speak the truth; for we were present at the betrothal of Joseph and Mary."

5. And Pilate called to him these twelve men who denied that he was born of fornication, and said to them: "I put you on your oath, by the safety of Caesar, that your statement is true, that he was not born of fornication." They said to Pilate: "We have a law, not to swear, because it is a sin. But let them swear by the safety of Caesar that it is not as we have said, and we will be worthy of death." Pilate said to Annas and Caiaphas: "Do you not answer these things?" And Annas and Caiaphas said to Pilate: "These twelve men are believed (who say) that he was not born of fornication. But we, the whole multitude, cry out that he was born of fornication, and is a sorcerer, and claims to be the Son of God and a king, and we are not believed." 6. And Pilate sent out the whole multitude, except the twelve men who denied that he was born of fornication, and commanded Jesus to be set apart. And he asked them: "For what cause do they wish to kill him?" They

answered Pilate: "They are incensed because he heals on the Sabbath." Pilate said: "For a good work do they wish to kill him?" They answered him: "Yes."

3. 1. And Pilate was filled with anger and went out of the praetorium and said to them: "I call the sun to witness that I find no fault in this man." The Jews answered and said to the governor: "If this man were not an evildoer, we would not have handed him over to you." And Pilate said: "Take him yourselves and judge him by your own law." The Jews said to Pilate: "It is not lawful for us to put any man to death." Pilate said: "Has God forbidden you to slay, but allowed me?"

2. And Pilate entered the praetorium again and called Jesus apart and asked him: "Are you the king of the Jews?" Jesus answered Pilate: "Do you say this of your own accord, or did others say it to you about me?" Pilate answered Jesus: "Am I a Jew? Your own nation and the chief priests have handed you over to me. What have you done?" Jesus answered: "My kingship is not of this world; for if my kingship were of this world, my servants would fight, that I might not be handed over to the Jews. But now is my kingship not from here." Pilate said to him: "So you are a king?" Jesus answered him: "You say that I am a king. For for this cause I was born and have come, that every one who is of the truth should hear my voice." Pilate said to him: "What is truth?" Jesus answered him: "Truth is from heaven." Pilate said: "Is there not truth upon earth?" Jesus said to Pilate: "You see how those who speak the truth are judged by those who have authority on earth."

4. 1. And Pilate left Jesus in the praetorium and went out to the Jews and said to them: "I find no fault in him." The Jews said to him: "He said: I am able to destroy this temple and build it in three days." Pilate said: "What temple?" The Jews said: "That which Solomon built in forty-six years; but this man says he will destroy it and build it in three days." Pilate said to them: "I am innocent of the blood of this righteous man; see to it yourselves." The Jews replied: "His blood be on us and on our children." 2. And Pilate called to him the elders and the priests and the Levites and said to them secretly: "Do not act thus; for nothing of which you have accused him deserves death. For your accusation concerns healing and profanation of the Sabbath." The elders and the priests and the Levites answered: "If a man blasphemes against Caesar, is he worthy of death or not?" Pilate said: "He is worthy of death." The Jews said to Pilate: "If a man blasphemes against Caesar, he is worthy of death, but this man has blasphemed against God."

3. Then the governor commanded the Jews to go out from the praetorium, and he called Jesus to him and said to him: "What shall I do with you?" Jesus answered Pilate: "As it was given to you." Pilate said: "How was it given?" Jesus said: "Moses and the prophets foretold my death and resurrection." The Jews had been eavesdropping and heard, and they said to Pilate: "What further need have you to hear of this blasphemy?" Pilate said to the Jews: "If this word is blasphemy, take him, bring him into your synagogue and judge him according to your law." The Jews answered Pilate: "It is contained in our law, that if a man sins against a man, he must receive forty strokes save one, but he who blasphemes against God must be stoned."

4. Pilate said to them: "Take him yourselves and punish him as you wish." The Jews said to Pilate: "We wish him to be crucified." Pilate said: "He does not deserve to be crucified." 5. The governor looked at the multitudes of the Jews standing around, and when he saw many of the Jews weeping, he said: "Not all the multitude wishes him to die." But the elders of the Jews said: "For this purpose has the whole multitude of us come, that he should die." Pilate said to the Jews: "Why should he die?" The Jews said: "Because he called himself the Son of God and a king."

5. 1. Now Nicodemus, a Jew, stood before the governor, and said: "I beseech you, honourable (governor), to allow me a few words." Pilate said: "Speak." Nicodemus said: "I said to the elders and the priests and the Levites and to all the multitude in the synagogue: What do you intend (to do) with this man? This man does many signs and wonders, which no one has done nor will do. Let him alone and contrive no evil against him. If the signs which he does are from God, they will stand; if they are from men, they will come to nothing. For Moses also, when he was sent by God into Egypt, did many signs which God commanded him to do before Pharaoh, king of Egypt. And there were there servants of Pharaoh, Jannes and Jambres, and they also did signs not a few which Moses did, and the Egyptians held them as gods, Jannes and Jambres. And since the signs which they did were not from God, they perished themselves and those who believed them. And now let this man go, for he does not deserve death."

2. The Jews said to Nicodemus: "You became his disciple and speak on his behalf." Nicodemus answered them: "Has the governor also become his disciple, and speaks on his behalf? Did not Caesar appoint him to this high office?" Then the Jews raged and gnashed their teeth against Nicodemus. Pilate said to them: "Why do you gnash your teeth against him, when you hear the truth?" The Jews said to

Nicodemus: "Receive his truth and his portion." Nicodemus said: "Amen, may it be as you have said."

6. 1. Then one of the Jews hastened forward and asked the governor that he might speak a word. The governor said: "If you wish to say anything, say it." And the Jew said: "For thirty-eight years I lay on a bed in anguish of pains, and when Jesus came many demoniacs and those lying sick of diverse diseases were healed by him. And certain young men took pity on me and carried me with my bed and brought me to him. And when Jesus saw me he had compassion, and spoke a word to me: Take up your bed and walk. And I took up my bed and walked." The Jews said to Pilate: "Ask him what day it was on which he was healed." He that was healed said: "On a Sabbath." The Jews said: "Did we not inform you so, that on the Sabbath he heals and casts out demons?" 2. And another Jew hastened forward and said: "I was born blind; I heard any man's voice, but did not see his face. And as Jesus passed by I cried with a loud voice: Have mercy on me, Son of David. And he took pity on me and put his hands on my eyes and I saw immediately." And another Jew hastened forward and said: "I was bowed, and he made me straight with a word." And another said: "I was a leper, and he healed me with a word."

7. 1. And a woman called Bernice crying out from a distance said: "I had an issue of blood and I touched the hem of his garment, and the issue of blood, which had lasted twelve years, ceased." The Jews said: "We have a law not to permit a woman to give testimony."

8. 1. And others, a multitude of men and women, cried out: "This man is a prophet, and the demons are subject to him." Pilate said to those who said the demons were subject to him: "Why are your teachers also not subject to him?" They said to Pilate: "We do not know." Others said: "Lazarus who was dead he raised up out of the tomb after four days." Then the governor began to tremble and said to all the multitude of the Jews: "Why do you wish to shed innocent blood?"

9. 1. And he called to him Nicodemus and the twelve men who said he was not born of fornication and said to them: "What shall I do? The people are becoming rebellious." They answered him: "We do not know. Let them see to it." Again Pilate called all the multitude of the Jews and said: "You know the custom that at the feast of unleavened bread a prisoner is released to you. I have in the prison one condemned for murder, called Barabbas, and this Jesus who stands before you, in whom I find no fault. Whom do you wish me to release to you?" But they cried out: "Barabbas." Pilate said: "Then what shall I

do with Jesus who is called Christ?" The Jews cried out: "Let him be crucified." But some of the Jews answered: "You are not Caesar's friend if you release this man, for he called himself the Son of God and a king. You wish him therefore to be king and not Caesar."

2. And Pilate was angry and said to the Jews: "Your nation is always seditious and in rebellion against your benefactors." The Jews asked: "What benefactors?" Pilate answered: "As I have heard, your God brought you out of Egypt out of hard slavery, and led you safe through the sea as if it had been dry land, and in the wilderness nourished you and gave you manna and quails, and gave you water to drink from a rock, and gave you the law. And despite all this you provoked the anger of your God: you wanted a molten calf and angered your God, and he wished to destroy you; and Moses made supplication for you, and you were not put to death. And now you accuse me of hating the emperor." 3. And he rose up from the judgment-seat and sought to go out. And the Jews cried out: "We know as king Caesar alone and not Jesus. For indeed the wise men brought him gifts from the east, as if he were a king. And when Herod heard from the wise men that a king was born, he sought to slay him. But when his father Joseph knew that, he took him and his mother, and they fled into Egypt. And when Herod heard it, he destroyed the children of the Hebrews who were born in Bethlehem."

4. When Pilate heard these words, he was afraid. And he silenced the multitudes, because they were crying out, and said to them: "So this is he whom Herod sought?" The Jews replied: "Yes, this is he." And Pilate took water and washed his hands before the sun and said: "I am innocent of the blood of this righteous man. You see to it." Again the Jews cried out: "His blood be on us and on our children." 5. Then Pilate commanded the curtain to be drawn before the judgment-seat on which he sat, and said to Jesus: "Your nation has convicted you of claiming to be a king. Therefore I have decreed that you should first be scourged according to the law of the pious emperors, and then hanged on the cross in the garden where you were seized. And let Dysmas and Gestas, the two malefactors, be crucified with you."

10. 1. And Jesus went out from the praetorium, and the two malefactors with him. And when they came to the place, they stripped him and girded him with a linen cloth and put a crown of thorns on his head. Likewise they hanged up also the two malefactors. But Jesus said: "Father, forgive them, for they know not what they do." And the soldiers parted his garments among them. And the people stood looking at him. And the chief priests and the rulers with them scoffed

at him, saying: "He saved others, let him save himself. If he is the Son of God, let him come down from the cross." And the soldiers also mocked him, coming and offering him vinegar with gall, and they said: "If you are the king of the Jews, save yourself." And Pilate after the sentence commanded the crime brought against him to be written as a title in Greek, Latin and Hebrew, according to the accusation of the Jews that he was king of the Jews.

2. One of the malefactors who were crucified said to him: "If you are the Christ, save yourself and us." But Dysmas answering rebuked him: "Do you not at all fear God, since you are in the same condemnation? And we indeed justly. For we are receiving the due reward of our deeds. But this man has done nothing wrong." And he said to Jesus: "Lord, remember me in your kingdom." And Jesus said to him: "Truly, I say to you, today you will be with me in paradise."

11. 1. And it was about the sixth hour, and there was darkness over the land until the ninth hour, for the sun was darkened. And the curtain of the temple was torn in two. And Jesus cried with a loud voice: "Father, baddach ephkid rouel," which means: "Into thy hands I commit my spirit." And having said this he gave up the ghost. And when the centurion saw what had happened, he praised God, saying: "This man was righteous." And all the multitudes who had come to this sight, when they saw what had taken place, beat their breasts and returned.

2. But the centurion reported to the governor what had happened. And when the governor and his wife heard, they were greatly grieved, and they neither ate nor drank on that day. And Pilate sent for the Jews and said to them: "Did you see what happened?" But they answered: "There was an eclipse of the sun in the usual way." 3. And his acquaintances had stood far off and the women who had come with him from Galilee, and saw these things. But a certain man named Joseph, a member of the council, from the town of Arimathaea, who also was waiting for the kingdom of God, this man went to Pilate and asked for the body of Jesus. And he took it down, and wrapped it in a clean linen cloth, and placed it in a rock-hewn tomb, in which no one had ever yet been laid.

12. 1. When the Jews heard that Joseph had asked for the body, they sought for him and the twelve men who said that Jesus was not born of fornication, and for Nicodemus and for many others, who had come forward before Pilate and made known his good works. But they all hid themselves, and only Nicodemus was seen by them, because he was a ruler of the Jews. And Nicodemus said to them: "How did you

enter into the synagogue?" The Jews answered him: "How did you enter into the synagogue? You are an accomplice of his, and his portion shall be with you in the world to come." Nicodemus said: "Amen, amen." Likewise also Joseph came forth (from his concealment?) and said to them: "Why are you angry with me, because I asked for the body of Jesus? See, I have placed it in my new tomb, having wrapped it in clean linen, and I rolled a stone before the door of the cave. And you have not done well with the righteous one, for you did not repent of having crucified him, but also pierced him with a spear."

Then the Jews seized Joseph and commanded him to be secured until the first day of the week. They said to him: "Know that the hour forbids us to do anything against you, because the Sabbath dawns. But know also that you will not even be counted worthy of burial, but we shall give your flesh to the birds of the heaven." Joseph answered: "This word is like that of the boastful Goliath, who insulted the living God and the holy David. For God said by the prophet: Vengeance is mine, I will repay, says the Lord. And now he who is uncircumcised in the flesh, but circumcised in heart, took water and washed his hands before the sun, saying: I am innocent of the blood of this righteous man. You see to it. And you answered Pilate: His blood be on us and on our children. And now I fear lest the wrath of God come upon you and your children, as you said." When the Jews heard these words, they were embittered in their hearts, and laid hold on Joseph and seized him and shut him in a building without a window, and guards remained at the door. And they sealed the door of the place where Joseph was shut up.

2. And on the Sabbath the rulers of the synagogue and the priests and the Levites ordered that all should present themselves in the synagogue on the first day of the week. And the whole multitude rose up early and took counsel in the synagogue by what death they should kill him. And when the council was in session they commanded him to be brought with great dishonour. And when they opened the door they did not find him. And all the people were astonished and filled with consternation because they found the seals undamaged, and Caiaphas had the key. And they dared no longer to lay hands on those who had spoken before Pilate on behalf of Jesus.

13. 1. And while they still sat in the synagogue and marvelled because of Joseph, there came some of the guard which the Jews had asked from Pilate to guard the tomb of Jesus, lest his disciples should come and steal him. And they told the rulers of the synagogue and the

priests and the Levites what had happened: how there was a great earthquake. "And we saw an angel descend from heaven, and he rolled away the stone from the mouth of the cave, and sat upon it, and he shone like snow and like lightning. And we were in great fear, and lay like dead men. And we heard the voice of the angel speaking to the women who waited at the tomb: Do not be afraid. I know that you seek Jesus who was crucified. He is not here. He has risen, as he said. Come and see the place where the Lord lay. And go quickly and tell his disciples that he has risen from the dead and is in Galilee."

2. The Jews asked: "To what women did he speak?" The members of the guard answered: "We do not know who they were." The Jews said: "At what hour was it?" The members of the guard answered: "At midnight." The Jews said: "And why did you not seize the women?" The members of the guard said: "We were like dead men through fear, and gave up hope of seeing the light of day; how could we then have seized them?" The Jews said: "As the Lord lives, we do not believe you." The members of the guard said to the Jews: "So many signs you saw in that man and you did not believe; and how can you believe us? You rightly swore: As the Lord lives. For he does live." Again the members of the guard said: "We have heard that you shut up him who asked for the body of Jesus, and sealed the door, and that when you opened it you did not find him. Therefore give us Joseph and we will give you Jesus." The Jews said: "Joseph has gone to his own city." And the members of the guard said to the Jews: "And Jesus has risen, as we heard from the angel, and is in Galilee." 3. And when the Jews heard these words, they feared greatly and said: "(Take heed) lest this report be heard and all incline to Jesus." And the Jews took counsel, and offered much money and gave it to the soldiers of the guard, saying: "Say that when you were sleeping his disciples came by night and stole him. And if this is heard by the governor, we will persuade him and keep you out of trouble."

14. 1. Now Phineës a priest and Adas a teacher and Angaeus a Levite came from Galilee to Jerusalem, and told the rulers of the synagogue and the priests and the Levites: "We saw Jesus and his disciples sitting upon the mountain which is called Mamilch. And he said to his disciples: Go into all the world and preach the gospel to the whole creation. He who believes and is baptized will be saved; but he who does not believe will be condemned. And these signs will accompany those who believe: in my name they will cast out demons; they will speak in new tongues; they will pick up serpents; and if they

drink any deadly thing, it will not hurt them; they will lay their hands on the sick and they will recover. And while Jesus was still speaking to his disciples, we saw him taken up into heaven."

2. Then the elders and the priests and the Levites said: "Give glory to the God of Israel, and confess before him if you indeed heard and saw what you have described." Those who told them said: "As the Lord God of our fathers Abraham, Isaac and Jacob lives, we heard these things and saw him taken up to heaven." The elders and the priests and the Levites said to them: "Did you come to tell us this, or did you come to offer prayer to God?" They answered: "To offer prayer to God." The elders and the chief priests and the Levites said to them: "If you came to offer prayer to God, to what purpose is this idle tale which you have babbled before all the people?" Phineës the priest and Adas the teacher and Angaeus the Levite said to the rulers of the synagogue and priests and Levites: "If the words which we spoke <concerning what we heard> and saw are sin, see, we stand before you. Do with us as it seems good in your eyes." And they took the law and adjured them to tell this no more to any one. And they gave them to eat and drink, and sent them out of the city, having given them money and three men to accompany them, and ordered them to depart as far as Galilee; and they went away in peace.

3. But when those men had departed to Galilee, the chief priests and the rulers of the synagogue and the elders assembled in the synagogue, and shut the gate, and raised a great lamentation, saying: "Why has this sign happened in Israel?" But Annas and Caiaphas said: "Why are you troubled? Why do you weep? Do you not know that his disciples gave much money to the guards of the tomb, <took away his body> and taught them to say that an angel descended from heaven and rolled away the stone from the door of the tomb?" But the priests and the elders replied: "Let it be that his disciples stole his body. But how did the soul enter again into the body, so that Jesus now waits in Galilee?" {But they, unable to give an answer, came with difficulty to say: "It is not lawful for us to believe the uncircumcised."}

15. 1. And Nicodemus stood up and stood before the council and said: "What you say is right. You know, people of the Lord, that the men who came from Galilee fear God and are men of substance, that they hate covetousness, and are men of peace. And they have declared on oath: We saw Jesus on the mountain Mamilch with his disciples. He taught them what you have heard from them. And we saw him (they said) taken up into heaven. And no one asked them in what manner he was taken up. Just as the holy scriptures tell us that Elijah

also was taken up into heaven, and Elisha cried with a loud voice, and Elijah cast his sheepskin cloak upon Elisha, and Elisha cast his cloak upon the Jordan, and crossed over and went to Jericho. And the sons of the prophets met him and said: Elisha, where is your master Elijah? And he said that he was taken up into heaven. But they said to Elisha: Has perhaps a spirit caught him up and cast him on one of the mountains? But let us take our servants with us and search for him. And they persuaded Elisha, and he went with them. And they searched for him for three days and did not find him, and they knew that he had been taken up. And now listen to me, and let us send to every mountain of Israel and see whether the Christ was taken up by a spirit and cast upon a mountain." And this proposal pleased them all. And they sent to every mountain of Israel, and searched for Jesus and did not find him. But they found Joseph in Arimathaea and no one dared to seize him.

2. And they told the elders and the priests and the Levites: "We went about to every mountain of Israel, and did not find Jesus. But Joseph we found in Arimathaea." And when they heard about Joseph, they rejoiced and gave glory to the God of Israel. And the rulers of the synagogue and the priests and the Levites took counsel how they should meet with Joseph, and they took a roll of papyrus and wrote to Joseph these words: "Peace be with you. We know that we have sinned against God and against you, and we have prayed to the God of Israel that you should condescend to come to your fathers and your children, because we are all troubled. For when we opened the door we did not find you. We know that we devised an evil plan against you; but the Lord helped you, and the Lord himself has brought to nothing our plan against you, honoured father Joseph."

3. And they chose from all Israel seven men who were friends of Joseph, whom also Joseph himself acknowledged as friends, and the rulers of the synagogue and the priests and the Levites said to them: "See! If he receives our letter and reads it, know that he will come with you to us. But if he does not read it, know that he is angry with us, and salute him in peace and return to us." And they blessed the men and dismissed them. And the men came to Joseph and greeted him with reverence, and said to him: "Peace be with you!" He replied: "Peace be with you and all Israel!" And they gave him the roll of the letter. Joseph took it and read it and kissed the letter, and blessed God and said: "Blessed be God, who has delivered the Israelites from shedding innocent blood. And blessed be the Lord, who sent his angel and sheltered me under his wings." And he set a table before them, and

they ate and drank and lay down there. 4. And they rose up early in the morning and prayed. And Joseph saddled his she-ass and went with the men, and they came to the holy city Jerusalem. And all the people met Joseph and cried: "Peace be to your entering in!" And he said to all the people: "Peace be with you!" And all kissed him, and prayed with Joseph, and were beside themselves with joy at seeing him. And Nicodemus received him into his house and made a great feast, and called the elders and the priests and the Levites to his house, and they made merry, eating and drinking with Joseph. And after singing a hymn each one went to his house; but Joseph remained in the house of Nicodemus.

5. And on the next day, which was the preparation, the rulers of the synagogue and the priests and the Levites rose up early and came to the house of Nicodemus. Nicodemus met them and said: "Peace be with you!" They answered: "Peace be with you and with Joseph and with all your house and with all the house of Joseph!" And he brought them into his house. And the whole council sat down, and Joseph sat between Annas and Caiaphas. And no one dared to speak a word to him. And Joseph said: "Why have you called me?" And they beckoned to Nicodemus to speak to Joseph. Nicodemus opened his mouth and said to Joseph: "Father, you know that the honourable teachers and the priests and the Levites wish information from you." Joseph answered: "Ask me." And Annas and Caiaphas took the law and adjured Joseph, saying: "Give glory to the God of Israel and make confession to him. For Achan also, when adjured by the prophet Joshua, did not commit perjury, but told him everything and concealed nothing from him. So do you also not conceal from us a single word." Joseph answered: "I will not conceal anything from you." And they said to him: "We were very angry because you asked for the body of Jesus, and wrapped it in a clean linen cloth, and placed it in a tomb. And for this reason we secured you in a house with no window, and locked and sealed the door, and guards watched where you were shut up. And on the first day of the week we opened it, and did not find you, and were much troubled, and all the people of God were amazed until yesterday. And now tell us what happened to you."

6. And Joseph said: "On the day of preparation about the tenth hour you shut me in, and I remained the whole Sabbath. And at midnight as I stood and prayed, the house where you shut me in was raised up by the four corners, and I saw as it were a lightning flash in my eyes. Full of fear I fell to the ground. And someone took me by the hand and raised me up from the place where I had fallen, and

something moist like water flowed from my head to my feet, and the smell of fragrant oil reached my nostrils. And he wiped my face and kissed me and said to me: Do not fear, Joseph. Open your eyes and see who it is who speaks with you. I looked up and saw Jesus. Trembling, I thought it was a phantom, and I said the (ten) commandments. And he said them with me. Now as you well know, a phantom immediately flees if it meets anyone and hears the commandments. And when I saw that he said them with me, I said to him: Rabbi Elijah! He said: I am not Elijah. And I said to him: Who are you, Lord? He replied: I am Jesus, whose body you asked for from Pilate, whom you clothed in clean linen, on whose face you placed a cloth, and whom you placed in your new cave, and you rolled a great stone to the door of the cave. And I asked him who spoke to me: Show me the place where I laid you. And he took me and showed me the place where I laid him. And the linen cloth lay there, and the cloth that was upon his face. Then I recognized that it was Jesus. And he took me by the hand and placed me in the middle of my house, with the doors shut, and led me to my bed and said to me: Peace be with you! Then he kissed me and said to me: Do not go out of your house for forty days. For see, I go to my brethren in Galilee."

16. 1. And when the rulers of the synagogue and the priests and the Levites heard these words from Joseph, they became as dead men and fell to the ground and fasted until the ninth hour. And Nicodemus and Joseph comforted Annas and Caiaphas and the priests and Levites, saying: "Get up and stand on your feet, and taste bread and strengthen your souls. For tomorrow is the Sabbath of the Lord." And they rose up and prayed to God, and ate and drank, and went each to his own house. 2. And on the Sabbath our teachers and the priests and the Levites sat and questioned one another, saying: "What is this wrath which has come upon us? For we know his father and his mother." Levi the teacher said: "I know that his parents fear God and do not withhold their prayers and pay tithes three times a year. And when Jesus was born, his parents brought him to this place, and gave God sacrifices and burnt offerings. And the great teacher Symeon took him in his arms and said: Lord, now lettest thou thy servant depart in peace, according to thy word; for mine eyes have seen thy salvation which thou hast prepared in the presence of all peoples, a light for revelation to the Gentiles, and for glory to thy people Israel. And Symeon blessed them and said to Mary his mother: I give you good tidings concerning this child. And Mary said: Good, my lord? And Symeon said to her: Good. Behold, this child is set for the fall and

rising of many in Israel, and for a sign that is spoken against—and a sword will pierce through your own soul also—that thoughts out of many hearts may be revealed."

3. They said to Levi the teacher: "How do you know this?" Levi answered them: "Do you not know that I learned the law from him?" The council said to him: "We wish to see your father." And they sent for his father. And when they questioned him, he said to them: "Why did you not believe my son? The blessed and righteous Symeon taught him the law." The council said: "Rabbi Levi, is the word true which you have spoken?" He answered: "It is true." Then the rulers of the synagogue and the priests and the Levites said among themselves: "Come, let us send to Galilee to the three men who came and told us of his teaching and of his being taken up, and let them tell us how they saw him taken up." And this word pleased them all. And they sent the three men who before had gone to Galilee with them, and said to them: "Say to Rabbi Adas and Rabbi Phineës and Rabbi Angaeus: Peace be with you and all who are with you. Since an important inquiry is taking place in the council, we were sent to you to call you to this holy place Jerusalem." 4. And the men went to Galilee and found them sitting and studying the law, and greeted them in peace. And the men who were in Galilee said to those who had come to them: "Peace be to all Israel." They answered: "Peace be with you." And again they said to them: "Why have you come?" Those who had been sent replied: "The council calls you to the holy city Jerusalem." When the men heard that they were sought by the council, they prayed to God and sat down at table with the men and ate and drank, and then arose and came in peace to Jerusalem.

5. And on the next day the council sat in the synagogue and questioned them, saying: "Did you indeed see Jesus sitting on the mountain Mamilch, teaching his eleven disciples? And did you see him taken up?" And the men answered them and said: "As we saw him taken up, so we have told you." 6. Annas said: "Separate them from one another, and let us see if their accounts agree." And they separated them from one another. And they called Adas first and asked him: "How did you see Jesus taken up?" Adas answered: "As he sat on the mountain Mamilch and taught his disciples, we saw that a cloud overshadowed him and his disciples. And the cloud carried him up to heaven, and his disciples lay on their faces on the ground." Then they called Phineës the priest and asked him also: "How did you see Jesus taken up?" And he said the same thing. And again they asked Angaeus, and he said the same thing. Then the members of the council said: "At

the mouth of two or three witnesses shall every matter be established."
Abuthem the teacher said: "It is written in the law: Enoch walked with
God, and was not, for God took him." Jairus the teacher said: "Also we
have heard of the death of the holy Moses, and we do not know how he
died. For it is written in the law of the Lord: And Moses died as the
mouth of the Lord determined, and no man knew of his sepulchre to
this day." And Rabbi Levi said: "Why did Rabbi Symeon say, when he
saw Jesus: Behold, this (child) is set for the fall and rising of many in
Israel, and for a sign that is spoken against?" And Rabbi Isaac said: "It
is written in the law: Behold, I send my messenger before your face.
He will go before you to guard you in every good way. In him my
name is named."

7. Then Annas and Caiaphas said: "You have rightly said what is
written in the law of Moses, that no one knows the death of Enoch and
no one has named the death of Moses. But Jesus had to give account
before Pilate; we saw how he received blows and spitting on his face,
that the soldiers put a crown of thorns upon him, that he was scourged
and condemned by Pilate and then was crucified at the place of a skull;
he was given vinegar and gall to drink, and Longinus the soldier
pierced his side with a spear. Our honourable father Joseph asked for
his body; and, he says, he rose again. And the three teachers declare:
We saw him taken up into heaven. And Rabbi Levi spoke and testified
to the words of Rabbi Symeon: Behold, this child is set for the fall and
rising of many in Israel, and for a sign that is spoken against." And all
the teachers said to all the people of the Lord: "If this is from the Lord,
and it is marvellous in your eyes, you shall surely know, O house of
Jacob, that it is written: Cursed is every one who hangs on a tree. And
another passage of scripture teaches: The gods who did not make the
heaven and the earth shall perish." And the priests and the Levites said
to one another: "If Jesus is remembered after fifty years, he will reign
for ever and create for himself a new people." Then the rulers of the
synagogue and the priests and the Levites admonished all Israel:
"Cursed is the man who shall worship the work of man's hand, and
cursed is the man who shall worship created things alongside the
creator." And the people answered: "Amen, amen."

8. And all the people praised the Lord God and sang: "Blessed be
the Lord who has given rest to the people of Israel according to all his
promises. Not one word remains unfulfilled of all the good which he
promised to his servant Moses. May the Lord our God be with us as he
was with our fathers. May he not forsake us. May he not let the will die
in us, to turn our heart to him, and walk in all his ways, and keep his

commandments and laws which he gave to our fathers. And the Lord shall be king over all the earth on that day. And there shall be one God and his name shall be one, our Lord and king. He shall save us. There is none like thee, O Lord. Great art thou, O Lord, and great is thy name. Heal us, O Lord, in thy power, and we shall be healed. Save us, Lord, and we shall be saved. For we are thy portion and inheritance. The Lord will not forsake his people for his great name's sake, for the Lord has begun to make us his people." After this hymn of praise they all departed, every man to his house, glorifying God. For his is the glory for ever and ever. Amen.

SELECT
ANNOTATED
BIBLIOGRAPHIES

The Gospel of Thomas

The papyrus fragments of the three different manuscripts of the Greek text of the *Gospel of Thomas* were first edited by Bernard P. Grenfell and Arthur S. Hunt in the following publications: Papyrus Oxyrhynchus i. 1: *LOGIA JESOU: Sayings of Our Lord* (London: Frowde, 1897) with two plates; Papyrus Oxyrhynchus iv. 654: *New Sayings of Jesus and Fragment of a Lost Gospel from Oxyrhynchus* (London: Frowde, 1904) with a plate; and Papyrus Oxyrhynchus iv. 655: *The Oxyrhynchus Papyri: Part IV* (London: Egypt Exploration Fund, 1904), 22–28, with Plate II. The Coptic text was first published by Antoine Guillaumont, Henri-Charles Puech, Gilles Quispel, Walter Till, and Yassah 'Abd al Masîḥ, *The Gospel According to Thomas* (Leiden: E. J. Brill; New York: Harper & Brothers, 1959). A splendid facsimile edition of the Coptic text was recently published under the auspices of the Department of Antiquities of the Arab Republic of Egypt, in conjunction with UNESCO: *The Facsimile Edition of the Nag Hammadi Codices: Codex II* (Leiden: E. J. Brill, 1974). A new critical edition of the Greek fragments by Harold W. Attridge, along with a new critical edition of the Coptic text by Bentley Layton, is currently in preparation for the series *The Coptic Gnostic Library* (Bentley Layton, *Nag Hammadi Codex II: CG II, 2-II, 7 together with XIII, 2*, Brit. Lib. Or. 4926(1), and P. Oxy. 1, 654, 655*, Nag Hammadi Studies [Leiden: E. J. Brill, forthcoming]). Excellent discussions of the text and its traditions may be found in the essays of James M. Robinson and Helmut Koester, *Trajectories Through Early Christianity* (Fortress Press, 1971).

The Dialogue of the Savior

The *Dialogue of the Savior* was published for the first time in a facsimile edition: *The Facsimile Edition of the Nag Hammadi Codices: Codex III* (Leiden: E. J. Brill, 1976). A critical edition is currently in preparation for the series *The Coptic Gnostic Library* by the members of the Coptic Gnostic Library Project of the Institute for Antiquity and Christianity, at Claremont. Some lost fragments of pages 145–146 of the *Dialogue of the Savior* were recently discovered at Yale University and published by Stephen Emmel, "A Fragment of Nag Hammadi Codex III in the Beinecke Library: Yale Inv. 1784," *Bulletin of the American Society of Papyrologists* 17 (1980), 53–60. A facsimile reproduction of the Yale papyrus is scheduled to appear in the section of additions and corrections in *The Facsimile Edition of the Nag Hammadi Codices: Introduction* (Leiden: E. J. Brill, forthcoming). A more detailed introduction to this document is given by Elaine Pagels and Helmut Koester, "Report on the *Dialogue of the Savior* (CG III, 5)," *Nag Hammadi and Gnosis: Papers read at the First International Congress of Coptology (Cairo, December 1976)*, Nag Hammadi Studies 14, ed. R. McL. Wilson (Leiden: E. J. Brill, 1978), 66–74.

The Gospel of the Egyptians

The best critical editions of the Greek text of the *Gospel of the Egyptians* are the following: for the *Stromateis*, that of Otto Stählin, *Clemens Alexandrinus 2: Stromata Buch I-VI*, Griechische christlichen Schriftsteller (Leipzig: Hinrichs, 1906); and for the *Excerpta ex Theodoto*, that of François Sagnard, *Extraits de Théodote*, Sources chrétiennes 23 (Paris: Editions du Cerf, 1948; reprinted, 1970). The finest discussion of the theological tradition of the text is that of Dennis Ronald MacDonald, *There Is No Male and Female: Galatians 3:26–28 and Gnostic Baptismal Tradition* (Unpublished Ph.D. dissertation, Harvard University, 1978).

Papyrus Oxyrhynchus 840

Papyrus Oxyrhynchus 840 was first published, in a critical edition, by Bernard P. Grenfell and Arthur S. Hunt, *The Oxyrhynchus Papyri: Part V* (London: Egypt Exploration Fund, 1908), 1–10, with Plate I. That same year another edition of the Greek text was made by Henry Barclay Swete, "Zwei neue Evangelienfragmente," Kleine Texte für Vorlesungen und Übungen 31, ed. Hans Lietzmann (Bonn: Marcus and Weber, 1908; reprinted, 1924), 3–9. The most recent edition and discussion, with slight alterations in the reading of the Greek text as edited by Swete, is that of Joachim Jeremias, *Unknown Sayings of Jesus*, 2d ed., trans. Reginald H. Fuller (London: S.P.C.K., 1964), 47–60, 104–105.

The Apocryphon of James

The *Apocryphon of James* was first published in a critical edition in French, with appended translations in German and English, by Michel Malinine, Henri-Charles Puech, Gilles Quispel, Walter Till, Rodolphe Kasser, R. McL. Wilson, and Jan Zandee, *Epistula Iacobi Apocrypha* (Zurich/Stuttgart: Rascher, 1968) with complete plates. A magnificent facsimile edition of the text has been recently published: *The Facsimile Edition of the Nag Hammadi*

Codices: Codex I (Leiden: E. J. Brill, 1977). A new critical edition is currently in preparation for the series *The Coptic Gnostic Library* by the members of the Coptic Gnostic Library Project of the Institute for Antiquity and Christianity, at Claremont: Harold W. Attridge, *Nag Hammadi Codex I (The Jung Codex)*, Nag Hammadi Studies (Leiden: E. J. Brill, forthcoming).

The Secret Gospel of Mark

The *Secret Gospel of Mark* was first published in a critical edition, with a facsimile, transcription, translation, and learned exposition, by Morton Smith, *Clement of Alexandria and a Secret Gospel of Mark* (Harvard University Press, 1973), 446–447, with Plates I-III. The most recent publication of the text is in an addendum to the critical edition of Clement of Alexandria by Ursula Treu, *Clemens Alexandrinus 4/1: Register*, Griechische christlichen Schriftsteller, 2d ed. (Berlin: Akademie-Verlag, 1980), xvii–xviii. The most recent discussion of the text is that of Helmut Koester, "History and Development of Mark's Gospel (From Mark to *Secret Mark* and 'Canonical' Mark)," *A Time for Reappraisal and Fresh Approaches: Colloquy on New Testament Studies*, ed. Bruce Corley (Mercer University Press, forthcoming).

Papyrus Egerton 2

Papyrus Egerton 2 was first published by H. Idris Bell and T. C. Skeat, *Fragments of an Unknown Gospel and Other Early Christian Papyri* (London: British Museum, 1935), 1–41, with Plates I and II. That very year a revised edition of the Greek text was published, with corrections, by the same authors: *The New Gospel Fragments* (London: British Museum, 1935; reprinted, 1951, 1955), with a plate. The best edition and discussion of the text is that of Goro Mayeda, *Das Leben-Jesu-Fragment Papyrus Egerton 2 und seine Stellung in der urchristlichen Literaturgeschichte* (Bern: Paul Haupt, 1946), 7–11.

The Gospel of Peter

The *Gospel of Peter* was first published by U. Bouriant, "Fragments du texte grec du livre d'Enoch et de quelques écrits attribués a Saint Pierre," *Mémoires publiés par les membres de la Mission archéologique française au Caire* 9/1 (Paris: Libraire de la Société asiatique, 1892), 137–142. A facsimile edition is bound together in that same volume, although it was published the next year by A. Lods, "Reproduction en héliogravure du manuscrit d'Enoch et des écrits attribués a Saint Pierre," *Mémoires publiés par les membres de la*

Mission archéologique française au Caire 9/3 (Paris: Libraire de la Société asiatique, 1893), 219–224, with Plates II-VI. The most recent critical edition is that of M. G. Mara, *Evangile de Pierre*, Sources chrétiennes 201 (Paris: Editions du Cerf, 1973). The fragments of Papyrus Oxyrhynchus xli. 2949, which correspond with the *Gospel of Peter* 2.3–5, have been published by R. A. Coles, *The Oxyrhynchus Papyri: Volume XLI* (London: Egypt Exploration Society, 1972), 15–16, with Plate II. A fine discussion of these fragments, which confirms their identification with the *Gospel of Peter*, has just been published by Dieter Lührmann, "P Ox 2949: EvPt 3–5 in einer Handschrift des 2./3. Jahrhunderts," *Zeitschrift für die neutestamentliche Wissenschaft* 72 (1981), 216–226.

The Gospel of the Hebrews

The fragments of the *Gospel of the Hebrews* are conveniently collected, in their original languages, in the following editions: Erwin Preuschen, "Reste des Hebräerevangeliums," *Antilegomena: Die Reste der ausserkanonischen Evangelien und urchristlichen Überlieferungen*, 2d ed. (Giessen: Töpelmann, 1905), 4–5, 8–9; Erich Klostermann, "Hebräerevangelium (Nazaräerevangelium)," *Apocrypha II: Evangelien*, Kleine Texte für Vorlesungen und Übungen 8, 3d ed., ed. Hans Lietzmann (Berlin: Walter de Gruyter, 1929), 5–10, 12; and A. F. J. Klijn and G. J. Reinink, *Patristic Evidence for Jewish-Christian Sects*, Supplements to Novum Testamentum 36 (Leiden: E. J. Brill, 1973), where the texts are collected, with English translations, under the names of the respective authors who cited them. The Coptic text of the fragment preserved in the writings of Cyril of Jerusalem may be found in E. A. Wallis Budge, *Miscellaneous Coptic Texts in the Dialect of Upper Egypt: Part I* (London: British Museum, 1915; reprinted, New York: AMS Press, 1977), 59–60.

"John's Preaching of the Gospel," The Acts of John 87–105

The identification of certain fragments of the proceedings of the Second Nicene Council of 787 as part of what is now called "John's Preaching of the Gospel" was first made by Johann Karl Thilo, "Colliguntur et commentariis illustrantur fragmenta actuum S. Ioannis a Leucio Charino conscriptorum: Particula prima," *Universitatis Literariae Fridericianae Halis consociatae programma paschale* (Halle, 1847), 14–17. The Vienna manuscript, which preserves the entirety of "John's Preaching of the Gospel," was first published by Montague Rhodes James, "Apocrypha anecdota: Second Series," Texts and Studies 5/1, ed. J. Armitage Robinson (Cambridge: Cambridge University Press, 1897), ix-xxviii, 2–25. The fragments quoted by Augustine in a letter to Ceretius (*Epistle* number 237) are published in a critical edition in *S. Aureli Augustini Hipponiensis episcopi epistulae: Pars IV*, Corpus scriptorum ecclesiasticorum latinorum 57/2, ed. Alois Goldbacher (Vienna: Tempsky/ Leipzig: Freytag, 1911), 526–532. The best critical edition of the Greek text of this section of the *Acts of John* is that of Maximilian Bonnet, "Acta Ioannis," *Acta apostolorum apocrypha*, 2 vols. in 3 parts, ed. Richard Adelbert Lipsius and Maximilian Bonnet (Leipzig: Mendelssohn, 1898; reprinted, Hildesheim: Georg Olms, 1959), 2/1. xxvi–xxxiii, 193–203.

The Gospel of the Nazoreans

The fragments of the *Gospel of the Nazoreans* are conveniently collected in the following editions: Erwin Preuschen, "Reste des Hebräerevangeliums," *Antilegomena: Die Reste der ausserkanonischen Evangelien und urchristlichen Überlieferungen*, 2d ed. (Giessen: Töpelmann, 1905), 4–7, 9; Erich Klostermann, "Hebräerevangelium (Nazaräerevangelium)," *Apocrypha II: Evangelien*, Kleine Texte für Vorlesungen und Übungen 8, 3d ed., ed. Hans Lietzmann (Berlin: Walter de Gruyter, 1929), 6–7, 10–12; and A. F. J. Klijn and G. J. Reinink, *Patristic Evidence for Jewish-Christian Sects*, Supplements to Novum Testamentum 36 (Leiden: E. J. Brill, 1973), where the texts may be found under the names of the respective authors who cited them. The Greek fragments of the "Zion Gospel" edition are collected by Alfred Schmidtke, *Neue Fragmente und Untersuchungen zu den judenchristlichen Evangelien*, Texte und Untersuchungen 37/1 (Leipzig: Hinrichs, 1911), 39–40.

The Gospel of the Ebionites

The fragments of the *Gospel of the Ebionites* are conveniently collected in the following editions: Erwin Preuschen, "Reste des Evangeliums der Ebioniten," *Antilegomena: Die Reste der ausserkanonischen Evangelien und urchristlichen Überlieferungen*, 2d ed. (Giessen: Töpelmann, 1905), 10–12; Erich Klostermann, "Ebionitenevangelium (Evangelium der Zwölf?)," *Apocrypha II: Evangelien*, Kleine Texte für Vorlesungen und Übungen 8, 3d ed., ed. Hans Lietzmann (Berlin: Walter de Gruyter, 1929), 13–14; and A. F. J. Klijn and G. J. Reinink, *Patristic Evidence for Jewish-Christian Sects*, Supplements to Novum Testamentum 36 (Leiden: E. J. Brill, 1973), 178–182, 188.

The Protevangelium of James

The first published edition of the Greek text of the *Protevangelium of James*, with an accompanying Latin translation, is that of Michael Neander, *Catechesis Martini Lutheri parua, graecolatina, postremum recognita* (Basel: Per Ioannem Oporinum, 1564), 356–392. A critical edition of seventeen manuscripts of the Greek text that were accessible before the twentieth century—and an edition still indispensable for scholarly research—is that of Constantin Tischendorf, *Evangelia apocrypha*, Editio altera (Leipzig: Mendelssohn, 1876), xii–xxii, 1–50. By far the most complete textual study is Boyd Lee Daniels' *The Greek Manuscript Tradition of the Protevangelium Jacobi*, 2 vols. in 3 parts (Unpublished Ph.D. dissertation, Duke University, 1956). He has examined eighty-one Greek manuscripts (of the one hundred thirty-eight known to him) and produced the best eclectic text available—based on nearly five times the number of manuscripts used by Tischendorf! The Bodmer papyrus from the third century, which unfortunately was not known when Daniels wrote his dissertation, was first published by Michel Testuz, *Papyrus Bodmer V: Nativité de Marie* (Cologny-Geneva: Bibliotheca Bodmeriana, 1958) with a plate. The most recent critical edition of the Greek text, giving special attention to the readings of the Bodmer papyrus, but also including a collation of some of the salient readings of other textual editions, including Tischendorf's, is that of Emile de Strycker, *La Forme la plus ancienne du Protévangile de Jacques*, Subsidia hagiographica 33 (Brussels: Société des Bollandistes, 1961), with a plate.

The Infancy Gospel of Thomas

The first portion of the *Infancy Gospel of Thomas* to be published in Greek, with an appended translation in Latin, was a fragment of what is now known to be part of the longer recension of the text. This fragment, which contains the first six chapters of the text, is preserved in a Paris manuscript that dates from the fifteenth century, and was published in a note to an edition of the *Apostolic Constitutions* by Jean Baptiste Cotelier, *SS. Patrum qui temporibus apostolicis floruerunt*, 2 vols. (Antwerp: Huguetanorum sumtibus, 1698), 1. 345–346. The best critical edition of both recensions of the Greek text is that of Constantin Tischendorf, *Evangelia apocrypha*, Editio altera (Leipzig: Mendelssohn, 1876), xxxvi–xlviii, 140–157 (the longer recension), 158–163 (the shorter recension). The Syriac text, with an English translation, was first published by W. Wright, *Contributions to the Apocryphal Literature of the New Testament* (London: Williams and Norgate, 1865), 6–17. The most recent discussion of the text is that of Stephen Gero, "The Infancy Gospel of

Thomas: A Study of the Textual and Literary Problems," *Novum Testamentum* 13 (1971), 46–80.

The Epistula Apostolorum

The Coptic text of the *Epistula Apostolorum* was first published by Carl Schmidt, *Gespräche Jesu mit seinen Jüngern nach der Auferstehung*, Texte und Untersuchungen 43 (Leipzig: Hinrichs, 1919; reprinted, Hildesheim: Georg Olms, 1967), 1*–26*, with a plate. The Ethiopic text was first published by Louis Guerrier, "Le Testament en Galilée de Notre-Seigneur Jésus-Christ," *Patrologia Orientalis* 9/3 (1913), 177–232. A fragmentary page from a Latin translation also survives in a codex that dates from the fifth or sixth century C.E. This fragment, which corresponds to chapters 12, 13, and 17 of the present edition of the text, was first published by Josef Bick, "Wiener Palimpseste," *Sitzungsberichte der philosophisch-historischen Klasse der kaiserlichen Akademie der Wissenschaften* 159/7 (Vienna, 1908), 97–99, with Plate IV.

The Acts of Pilate

The Greek text of the *Acts of Pilate*, with an accompanying Latin translation, was published for the first time as part of the *Gospel of Nicodemus* by Andreas Birch, *Auctarium codicis apocryphi N.T. Fabriciani: Fasciculus primus* (Copenhagen: Arntzen and Hartier, 1804), 1–105. The best critical edition of both recensions of the Greek text is that of Constantin Tischendorf, *Evangelia apocrypha*, Editio altera (Leipzig: Mendelssohn, 1876), liv-lxxvi, 210–286 (the longer recension), 287–332 (the shorter recension). A synopsis of these two recensions is available in Primus Vannutelli, *Actorum Pilati textus synoptici* (Rome: Apud auctorem, 1938).